Unstoppable BLACK WOMAN

SISTERHOOD EDITION

A Compilation by
Donna Izzard

Unstoppable Black Woman: Sisterhood Edition

Brand It Beautifully™ Book Designs at branditbeautifully.com
Editing by: Exact Writing Services

ISBN: 978-0-578-94624-5

Printed in the United States of America

Love Cella D.

A Compilation by Donna Izzard

TABLE OF CONTENTS

FOREWORD
Written by Visionary Author
Donna Izzard

*"When you know who you are and what you
can do, there is nothing that can stop you.
You become unstoppable."*
— Donna Izzard

This book is for black women who desire to hear
someone say they are worthy of success. It will teach
them how to be unstoppable and help them make the
right choices in their career, relationships, businesses,
and ministries.

When Black women learn how to be unstoppable,
they can model it for their daughters, granddaughters,
sisters, nieces, aunts, moms, and grandmothers.

Give yourself permission to be an Unstoppable Black
Woman (UBW). This book has the foundation for all
black women to empower themselves, grow in their
faith, and explore new opportunities. It's not selfish but
praiseworthy if you are looking for a path with other
unstoppable Black sisters that will encourage you along
your journey.

An amazing collection of prayers, letters, and stories from
successful black women who have been able to break
through barriers that society set before them, is worth
reading and remembering. This Sisterhood Edition will
forever change how you see yourself as both an individual
and a vital member of the African American community.

An Unstoppable Black Woman is embracing her B's
unapologetically: Black, Beautiful, Brilliant, BOLD and
Business-Minded. Unstoppable Black Woman, that's
me.

Join the Unstoppable Black Woman circle on Facebook.

Want to be featured in our next Unstoppable Black Woman edition? **Email us at support@unstoppableblackwoman.com**

Want to learn how to be a visionary author God's Way? God gave me a blueprint, I would love to teach you.

Need an inspiring, igniting and inviting mindset change speaker for your next event? **Email us at support@unstoppableblackwoman.com**

About the Visionary Author

Donna Izzard is passionate in developing Black Women to take their position in society by embracing their blackness, beauty, brilliance, boldness and being business-minded.

ALLISON DENISE ARNETT

———— ⓒⓖⓒⓖⓒⓖ ————

Unstoppable Story

> *"They were just trying to intimidate us,*
> *imagining that they could discourage us and*
> *stop the work. So I continued the work with*
> *even greater determination."*
> **— Nehemiah 6:9 NLT**

Nehemiah was unstoppable. On multiple occasions people tried to distract him from his mission to rebuild the walls. Repeatedly, they used scare tactics to destroy his progression. But it did not work. He repeatedly told them "I can't come down." To me, that's what it means to be unstoppable. I might want to come down and address your attempts. I certainly am able to come down and spend my precious time going back and forth with you but no, I can't come down. This is the type of tenacious spirit we must grab ahold of.

Why? Like Nehemiah said, we are "doing a great work." In other words, it's bigger than us. It is highly important to God, to the purpose which He has set forth in our lives, and to the people who will be affected by our actions. When I was wrongfully terminated from my job one week after giving birth to my third child I could have let anger deter God's plans. I could have allowed single motherhood of three young children to keep me from committing to my business. I could have let the negative comments from people I love discourage my progress. Instead "I continued the work with even greater determination." It is with this brief introduction to my unstoppable story that I encourage you to embrace your beautiful, unstoppable self and finish the great work God has started in you.

Letter to My Younger Self

You know you've got this right? I need you to not question that. You prayed and you heard God's voice. You were not mistaken. Some days will be a breeze and other days you will want to quit, but don't. Ever. Instead, learn to rest when you are tired. Set boundaries and reassess them when you feel overwhelmed. The road will get clearer as you move forward. I'm not saying you'll have all the answers but in every moment, at every turn you will have everything you need. God is making sure of that. And because you are doing a great work for Him, you can not fail. Only believe and keep going. Oh... and do that big, scary thing.... it'll be worth it. I promise. I love you, Queen.

Prayer

Oh Lord, our God. How excellent is Your name in all the earth. My mind is still sometimes amazed at the thought that You are mindful of me; at how intimately You know me. And how tenacious you've made me in the pursuit of accomplishing my work for You. Continue to guide me, Lord. Remain at the center of my desires. Shine forth through the determination of my actions. Show yourself mighty in my life. Then help me to beautifully articulate the words to tell my unstoppable story so that it may honor You and make You even more believable to anyone who may question it. Keep me safe and joyful in Your unstoppable love. In Jesus' name I pray. Amen.

A Compilation by Donna Izzard

About the Author

Allison Denise is a Best Selling Author, International Speaker, and Award-Winning Graphic Designer of beautiful boss brands and books through her biz Brand It Beautifully™. A servant leader at heart and an eclectic, creative soul, she seeks to help Christian women in business stir up their gifts, monetize their message, edify the Body, and leave their legacy in the world. As an avid advocate of self-acceptance and spiritual empowerment it is her desire that every woman finds the power in their voice and the beauty in her story. Every book she publishes, event she hosts, or class she teaches is part of her vision from God to merge ministry and the marketplace into one. She prays that something you experience, someone you meet, or something you do as a result of this encounter will ignite the fire in you to Empower Your Inner Creator™ and become everything God designed you to be.

Connect on Instagram and Facebook @ImAllisonDenise
On the Web www.AllisonDeniseMinistries.com

A Compilation by Donna Izzard

ANGELINE HAMILTON-WILLIAMS

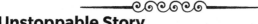

Unstoppable Story

We all go through trials and tribulations but falling down and not staying down is what makes you unstoppable. Being born an only child gave me a strong sense of self, and leadership. I am a born fighter. I never give up, an attribute that shined through my grandmother.

My fighting spirit was really tested in the workplace. Being the only woman of color for many years had its own challenges. In 2009, my livelihood was threatened at my job. False allegations involving firearms were made by coworkers. What ensued next was a lengthy investigation that could have resulted in charges being filed against me. A few years later, I was passed over for promotions. I discovered I was blacklisted because I chose solitude in a toxic environment. I was being spiritually attacked. I had two choices at this point: jump ship or stand tall; I chose the latter.

These adversities were sent to discourage me. I held my head high, forgave my accusers and allowed God to work in my life. What was supposed to be a setback created unstoppable opportunities for a comeback. My top workplace scriptures were Psalms 110:1 and 23:5. The position that I thought I needed, God said, "No, I have something better, and you are the chosen vessel to tell people about me." Since then, I have become the CEO of two of God's businesses while still on assignment awaiting God's exit strategy. Trust in the Lord with all of your heart. Don't lean on your own understanding.

Letter to My Younger Self

My Dear Angeline,

Life won't be easy but God will give you the strength you need. You may have to figure many things out by yourself but you'll do great. You'll go through a period in life where you'll encounter many obstacles. You'll be fine. You're unstoppable so you'll keep going no matter what. Your grandmother's prayers will always protect you. You got this! "Be strong and courageous. Do not be afraid. Do not be discouraged for the Lord God will be with you wherever you go." Joshua 1:8-9

Prayer

Educated. Beautiful. Worthy. Strong. That's you. Keep God first with everything you set your mind to do. Critics, noise, adversity - all those things will come but never forget these significant words, God's will be done. He said He'll never leave us and this I know is true. He walked with me through everything; He'll do the same for you. Our Father wants the best for us you have to understand when going through the trials in life. He always has your hand Faith is the belief of things that we can not see. I'm a living testimony because He's never left me. Be the Unstoppable Black Woman, He created you to be. Remind yourself everyday there's nothing that can stop you. The journey is never easy. Always do your best. When you can't, don't worry; He will do the rest. Look to the Lord and His strength. Seek His face always. 1 Chronicles 16:11

A Compilation by Donna Izzard

About the Author

Born and raised in Hartford, CT to Jamaican parents, Angeline Hamilton-Williams identified her affinity for writing from a young age. Growing up, Angeline felt her verbal expression was suppressed, and that she was perceived as aggressive every time she spoke. She wanted to be heard without being misjudged. As a result, Angeline turned to her natural talent of writing as a creative outlet and a way of expressing her thoughts.

In this book, she makes her voice heard through her incredible authorial prowess, and proves why she is an unstoppable black woman. Angeline is a CEO of two of God's businesses, a loving wife and mother of two adult sons. In her spare time, she enjoys traveling the world, reading, and me time.

You can engage her via Info@startwithhim.com

A Compilation by Donna Izzard

CAROLYN MIDDLETON

Unstoppable Story

The summer days of my youth were spent with my siblings, carefree and fun. As I got older, I became more aware of a divide between my neighbors in Leeds, AL, who all looked like me, and the Caucasian residents across the tracks, though I was unable to grasp why. Starting school, the stark difference in how we were treated was clear. Something was definitely not right.

The school bus that chauffeured the white children to and from school did not stop on our streets. There was no transportation provided for the children of color. I once asked my grandmother why people of color were treated differently. She told me: *"Things aren't always fair, but don't worry. Always know who* ***you*** *are, and remember it's not where you are right now, but where you are going that counts!"*

So I did not allow the racial disparities to stop me. I found the Lord at the age of seven. I persevered through primary school, middle school, and graduated with honors from high school with plans to continue my studies in the Fall. I was quickly immersed in college classes and work study, realizing that I could accomplish anything I set my mind to as per *Philippians 4:13*.

Soon after, my employment with United Airlines allowed me to see the world and work an amazing career while raising my family. After much travel I moved back to Alabama where I started baking for family, friends, and church functions. I soon realized the potential for my newest enterprise and envisioned becoming an entrepreneur. My grandmother's words, still with me, still driving me: *"It's not where you are right now, but where you are going that counts!"* **Cakes by Chris** was birthed. We are ALL given a portion of greatness. You don't have to wait for your dreams. Mishandled dreams will stunt your growth.

Letter to My Younger Self

Dear Younger Self,

If only I had known these things when I was your age. Let's take a stroll down memory lane. In our world, life was simple until we hit the double digits. Around age thirteen the goal was simply to fit in. What appeared so hard to comprehend then taught you the most powerful life lesson you could learn: be yourself no matter what; true gems always stand out! You are perfect the way God designed you. You're an intelligent woman, full of integrity, creativity, and you are beautiful, flaws and all. Life is an adventure filled with lessons that shape you into the queen you are! Trust your journey, follow God's lead. Live with no regrets. Chase your dreams and have that awesome life you deserve! Love, Your Older Self.

Prayer

Lord, thank you for enabling me to be strong, courageous and have the boldness to move forward becoming the unstoppable woman you have designed me to be. As you move before me, I will continue to follow the path you designed without fear or apprehension. Thank you for a heart of submission, obedience and an ear to hear and recognize Your voice. A godly mind that moves to the rhythm of your voice. It's Your grace and intervention that's connected me with an awesome group of unstoppable black women on a mission to empower and pour into other women by actions, deeds, and words. Amen

A Compilation by Donna Izzard

About the Author

Carolyn was born in Markeeta, Alabama on Friday March 29th, 1946. At a young age, her parents, Jake and Velma Bennet, saw potential in Carolyn that was much larger than their small town. In 1950, the family moved upstate to Leeds, Alabama for better educational opportunities. Carolyn is a graduate of R.R. Moton High School in 1964, and pursued a degree in Business Education from Wenona State College. She then spent over 25 years working for United Airlines until retirement in 2002. After retirement, she spent some time in the nursing program at Lawson State. Carolyn is a woman of many talents and wears many hats that have allowed her to attain much success over her lifetime. She is the mother of two children that have blessed her with six grandchildren and two great grandchildren. She attributes her sincere love for people, willingness to serve, hospitable nature, and love for cooking to her roots and relationship with God. Carolyn is now the CEO of **Cakes by Chris**, best known for its cakes, pies, and other tasty desserts in Leeds, where she currently resides.

A Compilation by Donna Izzard

CHARLEASE MCCAULEY-HATCHETT

---⚬⚬⚬⚬⚬---

Unstoppable Story

Looking at the word unstoppable leads me to question the true definition of the word. According to the Oxford dictionary it means impossible to stop or prevent. To be unstoppable, one must have a discerning spirit, not operating with an earthly perspective but from a Godly perspective. In this way of thinking, one is fueled by the Spirit that dwells within based on truth. Our focus should never be on temporal things, but on how to fulfill the mission and purpose God has set in your bones.

Be truthful to who you are and to Who created you. Many are confused over their identity. As a result, they are stifled in their walk and productivity. Look at your skin and know the melanin (blackness) was designed by God Himself. He imparts a level of boldness in each of us and empowers it for our good. Beauty comes from the Creator and I am beautiful in His eyes. My brilliance is not dependent upon how others perceive me. It comes from being true to myself and from always being in a posture to learn.

One aspect of learning comes from failing. We all fail in something because we are not perfect. I will let the totality of my existence manifest in the business-minded perspective I aim to fulfill, and roll with it. God created me to be impossible to be stopped or prevented in the blessings, plans and purpose He created for me. Thus, I am an Unstoppable Black Woman. That is me.

Letter to My Younger Self

Life is stress, struggle, & strain, BUT God has your future in His hands. Charlease, you remember walking into the viewing room of the funeral home and not recognizing dad in the coffin when you were 11 years old? You became angry and determined. You spoke aloud to God that night stating, "I'm going to make something of my life." That loss created a layer of stress that you were not prepared for and the devastation would follow you for the next 10 years. It did something to your psyche and followed you into your marriage. I know you struggled for a time till you gave your life to the Lord fully as an adult in your late 20's. Life is hard when you do not see your worth. No one told you how your blackness was a gift from God. People mistake your boldness for arrogance. Your blackness is deemed a threat, your beauty is used against you, and your brilliance can never shine if you are blocked in your thoughts and feelings towards others. Your worth is based on who created you not who berated you. God created you and has covered and blessed you. Rejoice! Your journey is not yet complete. You are loved. Continue to walk in your purpose.

Prayer

I lift my hands to Adoni, thanking Him for His gift of restoration through His son, Jesus Christ. You have been given special blessings of anointing, power, and prayer through the sacrificial blood of the Lamb. Open yourself up to be a channel for the purpose and plans He has specifically for you. The scripture says you have been chosen by the Father, made holy by the Spirit of God, and cleansed by the blood of the Son. What a beautiful blessing this is. Receive this in your spirit and walk into your purpose and calling, boldly recognizing your blackness created by Elohim. Your beauty, boldness, and brilliance is imparted in you by El Elyon. Enjoy the manifested wealth that will come from your business mind. Thank you, Jehovah Jireh, our provider. All glory, honor, and praise to Jehovah Rohi, our Shepherd. Amen

About the Author

Charlease McCauley Hatchett is an international bible study teacher, - A Co-Author in The Ultimate Faith Based Entrepreneur's Guide Lift Launch, Lead, and Non-Hodgkin's Large B Cell Lymphoma cancer survivor of 6 years. For over 25 years, she has been engaged and devoted in bringing people closer to the word of God as well as devoting her time to volunteering for various causes. She is a former volunteer with Precept Ministries as well as an international women's retreat coordinator, public speaker, and bible study leader. More recently, she became an entrepreneur and founded God is Bigger Than Ministries and is the current CEO. In the cancer space, as a survivor, Charlease wanted to equip and support those going through their cancer journey, so she created the Combat Ready Cancer Ministry Program at Fallbrook Church in Houston, TX and is the founder and CEO of Connected Through Cancer Foundation, a 501(c) 3 organization.

Charlease received her B.S. degree from Longwood University in Virginia. She currently resides in Spring, TX with her husband J. Harold Hatchett, III and has two adult children.

Website: www.godisbiggerthanministries.com or
http://connectedthroughcancer.org
Email: chahatchett@gmail.com ctcf@gmail.com

A Compilation by Donna Izzard

CHARLENE PRITCHETT STEVENSON

Unstoppable Story

I am now 57 years old, and in looking back over my life, I thought I would share with you a few of the lessons I learned along the way. I am thankful and grateful for the life that I have. It has had hills and valleys; highs and lows; and more joy than sadness.

My favorite thing was playing school and being the teacher. My flowers were my students. This was my imaginary world. Life is a teacher. My mother died when I was 21 years old, and I was not prepared to grow up overnight. Life taught me to keep moving and striving. I spent so much time working to have the American Dream, that I did not see the nightmare it really was. The dream took me away from precious moments with my son, husband, and all of those that I am close to. Yes, I bought the house, the car and lived in the suburbs. I did not have a white picket fence because it did not appeal to me. I set financial goals for myself and achieved them. It was still not enough.

Three years ago, my life made a shift, and I had a purpose. I finally realized my purpose and it changed my perspective. My gift is service and a heart for my young people. My company, ICLyte, was born. It is an organization designed to lift young adults to empowerment. My passion came from the love received from the elders.

Letter to My Younger Self

Dear Younger Charlene,

You are beautiful, gifted, and unstoppable. God has already equipped you with everything you need to be successful. Tap into your faith and allow God to use you. Life will teach you many things. I just need you to believe in you. Take time to breathe, for life is short. I wasted so much time accumulating things. Learn to love and appreciate everything. Even in the hard lessons there is good. They teach you endurance. I am now living my best life. I love, and I serve with grace, style, peace and much joy. Love, Older Charlene

Prayer

Father of the Living God we come humble as we know how. Thanking you for the gift of unstoppable women. It is your grace that enables us to keep striving and believing in the gift of life, you gave each of us. I come to you on behalf of my UBW sisters who stand in need of your guidance, grace and mercy. We stand on the backs of our ancestors, who paved the way that we would have the ability to be bold, brilliant and game changers. Father, please continue to give us the strength, vision and direction to continue to open doors for those who will come behind us. Let the work of our hands and hearts be for Your glory. May the fruits of Your Spirit reign true in us. We speak love over a world that needs a touch from You, Oh Lord. Amen

About the Author

Charlene Pritchett Stevenson has undergone a lot of sharpening that paved the way to be in the place where she is right now. After losing her mother at the age of twenty-one, Charlene pressed forward and graduated college with her master's degree in Health Service Administration. She was living the "American dream" – a loving family, friends, good government job, a home in the suburbs. But there was something missing. A few years ago, the idea came to her and her good friend Iris to start a mentorship organization, ICLyte, LLC. Charlene is doing her heart's desire and using the God given talent to guide and mentor young people. Charlene is the perfect example of an unstoppable black woman - wife to Bruce Levern Stevenson and mother to James Andrew Pritchett. She is Aunt Char, Grandma Char, a sister, friend, aunt, mentor, prayer warrior, Proverbs 31 woman, and most importantly, she is the daughter of the King.

A Compilation by Donna Izzard

CYNTHIA FOX EVERETT

Unstoppable Story

I am a mother of four and a grandmother of eight. I am an Army veteran of fourteen years. I survived six months in Desert Shield/Storm. I've been hospitalized with mental illness six times due to PTSD(post traumatic stress disorder) depression, suicide, MST(military sexual trauma). I survived domestic violence for nine years. I've also been delivered from an Opioid addiction since 2008. I had two mental breakdowns and felt like I had lost my mind but God was there to catch it! My mind slowly slipped through my fingers but God caught it.

I've developed resilience and endurance to deal with life and all that it has offered me thus far. By using my life's challenges, I'm able to adapt to change. I've kept God first and foremost in my life. No matter what has come my way I have stood on the principles of God. With Him, I have persisted through life's storms. Mental exhaustion, dealing with stigma and abuse almost choked the life out of me but I'm determined to win at any cost. I learned to show up for myself and to become an active participant in my life and my mental health care. I believe that my foundation of purpose is greater than my foundation of pain. I know now that my silence almost killed me. I now advocate for all that God has delivered me from and through. I found my purpose through life's trials and I'm blessed.

Letter to My Younger Self

Dear Cynthia,

Congratulations on overcoming every inherited generational obstacle given to you as a blanketed concrete birthright. You weren't given permission to detour from your legacy. Thank you for seeking God and finding an infallible partner to assist and guide you in writing and rewriting your own life's lessons and reversing the conditional birthright given to you. You have shuffled the deck of cards handed to you by life. You refused to fold with the hand you were dealt. You are determined to win at any cost. Please continue to demolish all barriers and obstacles. I love you and I am very proud of you! With Earned Respect, Yourself

Prayer

I pray that God continues to be your divine guide. May you forgive yourself unselfishly. Welcome grace with an open heart. Face each day with victory and confidence. Renew your mind daily and learn to refresh your soul so that your spirit will be refreshed and renewed. Learn to preserve yourself so that you are able to support others. Reward yourself for every achievement. Show yourself the same grace and mercy as you show others. Love yourself unconditionally in spite of your perfect imperfections. Always guide your thoughts and words and actions towards the path of peace and love. Strengthen your spirit to endure life's lessons in and out of season. May you be draped with strength to endure life's storms effortlessly. In all things use wisdom and understanding before you make decisions concerning others' and yourself. You will be strengthened to persist through life's storms. Many blessings to you.

A Compilation by Donna Izzard

About the Author

Cynthia Fox Everett is a mother of four, grandmother of eight. She is a U.S. Army veteran of fourteen years. She has an associate degree in Criminal Justice and furthered her education at Shaw University. She rededicated her life to Christ in 2003 and accepted the mission and the responsibility to serve in the house of the Lord. She wants to empower and inspire others to seek Jesus and find the strength to heal so that they have the courage to rewrite their future, tell their story, and help others heal. She is also a certified life coach and a Bestselling Co-Author of Amazon's *Souled Out* and *Souled Out Volume 2*, *Soul Talk Volume 2*, *Soul Talk Volume 3* and *Soulful Affirmations* with **Cheryl Polote-Williamson** as the visionary. She is also a bestselling co-author with visionary **Venessa D. Abram, MBA**, in *The Voices Behind Mental. Illness Series 2*, and *The Life of a Soldier, Series 5*. She is a member of NAMI, an advocate for domestic violence and a survivor, also a Mental Health advocate.

To connect email her at cynthiaeverett8@gmail.com

A Compilation by Donna Izzard

DAVINA CARTER WILSON

Unstoppable Story

Every chapter of my life speaks Unstoppable Black Woman. From the struggles I've had during my divorce, to being a single mother raising three proud men, my journey in life has propelled me to have the courage, grit, wisdom and strength to not only survive but thrive.

Being black, a woman, and a single parent are all supposed to be deal breakers for an aspiring entrepreneur. Conventional wisdom has always supported the exact opposite, and held that up to be the necessary criteria in order to have success. But not for me. I used every pain, every struggle, every obstacle to nurture myself and give me the confidence to aim higher beyond what society dictates or expects.

Every fiber of my being screams Unstoppable Black Woman. With one of my sons being incarcerated, it took every ounce of my physical strength, emotional stability and mental fortitude to help and guide him in getting his life back on track. In 2020, I started a support group for mothers with sons in prison to give support and guidance through difficult times.

Every corner of my mind is filled with the ideas and creativity of an Unstoppable Black Woman. As the Founder of Davina Coaching & Consulting LLC, being a Fitness Instructor, Health & Wellness Coach, and a trainer for speakers, I've learned so much through my work and business experience and this has allowed me to branch out and undertake various new projects. My latest venture is launching a stylish eyewear collection, Divine Vision Frames, which has sold out multiple times in a variety of locations.

I AM an Unstoppable Black Woman.

Letter to My Younger Self

Young Davina,

True to your name, you have the heavenly blessing and capacity to achieve whatever you want to pour your heart and soul into. And you will! Stay strong and stand firm. You will encounter roadblocks along the way. The path isn't always smooth and easy, but your divine determination will get you through the worst of times. The worst will become your best. The weaknesses you thought you have, you will wear them proudly as a badge of honor, signifying every hurdle and hardship you have successfully overcome in life. Brace yourself, young Davina. Both the best and the worst are yet to come, and these will form the perfect balance that will pave the way to shaping you into the amazing Unstoppable Black Woman into which you will blossom. Do not waver in your faith. Believe in yourself. And eagerly await what lies ahead.

Prayer

My dear sister and fellow Unstoppable Black Woman, despite what the world or cultural norm tells you, you have everything it takes to thrive, be successful, and live abundantly. Whatever you put your mind into, you are an unstoppable force to be reckoned with. Do not allow yourself to be limited by your environment, resources, family background, or current circumstances. These are mere stepping stones that will bring you closer to the goal you've set for yourself. You have every right to be the bright, successful woman you see yourself to be. Do not merely aspire for it - do it. Achieve it. By the grace of God, you can maximize yourself as and be the empowered, successful woman you are destined to be. Hold on to faith that you will reach your destination, and do not forget to pass on this wisdom to the generation of Unstoppable Black Women of the future.

A Compilation by Donna Izzard

About the Author

Davina Carter Wilson is the founder of Davina Coaching and Consulting which helps people activate the power within and this is Davina's passion. She is a Fitness Instructor, Health & Wellness Coach, and a trainer for speakers.

She is a multi-award winning trailblazer in her field, having made significant contributions to the training, health and coaching sectors. Her most notable awards and recognitions include the 2018 Healthier Hero Award, 2019 Health & Wellness Award for ACHI Magazine, 2018 Mentor for D.A.P.I. of Delaware, and 2018-2019 TED Talk Speaker.

Aside from her professional and entrepreneurial ventures, Davina stays actively involved in non-profit organizations such as being appointed as the Vice-President of (SGS) Sister Growing Strong. With no women left behind.

Davina's most recent ventures include starting a support group for mothers with imprisoned children, and launching a hot new eyewear collection, Divine Vision Frames.

Davina is from Claymont, Delaware and the proud mother of three sons and loving grandmother to two grandchildren.

Get in touch with Davina:
- davinaelise6@gmail.com
- divinevisionframes@gmail.com
- divine-vision-frames.myshopify.com

A Compilation by Donna Izzard

DENISE V. CLIATT

———— ᏭᏭᏭᏭᏭᏭ ————

Unstoppable Story

I've always wanted to be a mom. I'd often tell my friends, "I am believing in God for a husband and three sons whose worlds revolve around me." Things haven't gone as I expected!

At the age of 44 I embarked on motherhood through adoption as a single woman. I attended an adoption seminar at an agency in Cherry Hill, NJ. A few weeks later I submitted my application and began the process. I had to be FBI fingerprinted, provide personal and work recommendations, submit my bank accounts and pay statements, do numerous classes and have a home study. The last step was to film a video and create a written profile. In May 2011, I was officially waiting to be matched!

On August 24, 2011, I was in my office when my cell phone rang. It was my social worker; she called to tell me that *my* son (remember, I always wanted sons) was born the night before and I had to get to Philadelphia because he was being discharged to me the NEXT DAY! I will never forget that call. It was truly one of the most amazing days of my life. My son's middle name, Samuel, is from the bible, which means, ***asked from God.*** It is from the story of Hannah. 1 Samuel 1:20 states that Hannah named her first born, Samuel, saying, "Because I asked the Lord for him."

I was *BOLD TO BELIEVE* for the manifestation of motherhood! God has a plan. It's our responsibility to trust Him as it unfolds!

Letter to My Younger Self

Dearest Denise,

Things won't go exactly how you planned but oh, does God have some marvelous blessings stored up for you! Know that you'll feel His presence during your darkest days and during your highest highs. Trust that voice inside of you when it's telling you, "you can do it!" Talk back when the wrong voice tells you things that don't lift you up! Don't spend one second of time comparing yourself to others. God made you to run YOUR race! Go get it Girl!

Prayer

Father God,

Thank you for the Unstoppable Black Woman Movement! Thank you for making me a Black, Bold, Brilliant, Business-minded and Beautiful woman! Allow me to embrace ALL of my "B's"! Thank you for impressing upon me to pray BOLD prayers and to believe YOUR promises! Thank you that my BEST days are ahead of me! As I enter into this new season in my life let me not give in to doubt or fear but instead *ONLY BELIEVE!*

B – Believe
O – On
L – Living
D- Dreams

About the Author

Denise Vernell Cliatt is a seasoned Human Resources professional and new Entrepreneur. She worked at Prudential Financial for over 30 years in roles in Finance and Human Resources. In 2020, Denise entered entrepreneurship and became an independent consultant with Beautycounter, a CLEAN beauty brand whose mission is to get safer personal care products into the hands of everyone. A woman of faith, Denise is a leader in her church, a member of Delta Sigma Theta Sorority, Incorporated and serves on the board of Currently Trending.

A former foster mom, Denise is passionate about adoption and foster care. Denise and her son Julian reside in Somerset, New Jersey with their Blue Heeler rescue dog, Spring.

A Compilation by Donna Izzard

ERICA D. TOUSSAINT

Unstoppable Story

I always wanted something *different*... something more than average. This is not to say that I thought I was better than anyone else; as a matter of fact, it was just the opposite. At times, when I was growing up, I used to feel so insecure. One thing for sure - I didn't like my voice and didn't believe I would ever have anything of value to offer the world. Experiencing childhood trauma surely didn't make things any better. Battered, broken and bruised, I started my tumble through this thing called life.

Today, I stand in awe, wonder and absolute amazement as I watch God use a small-town country girl with more baggage than one could imagine. A real "bag lady". He turned that insecurity into my Superpower. My voice; can you believe that? I use my voice daily to bring light, joy and hope to the lives of people at their wits end and ready to quit on everything. Speaking words that resonate with them, love on them, allow them to pour out their hurts and heart, I even go so far as to pray with them. Reminding some and informing others of just how incredible, awesome, and wonderful they are and how they should give themselves and God just one more chance. Only Believe!

It took several years before I began to realize that the Creator was utilizing my insecurities and experiences for the incubation of my genius and what I have now embraced as my own unique brand of unstoppable.

Letter to My Younger Self

Dear Younger Me,

I know this letter is alarming. Your older self is penning a letter to you. How spooky is that? I've peaked into your future; things turn out wonderful. Here is what you must do: (1) apply the Balm of Gilead to every trauma you encounter; (2) embrace your beauty (specifically that mole you despise; your future Boaz loves it); (3) keep your say/do ratio high; (4) speak up - your voice is your victory over insecurities and circumstances for your Elohvation; (5) stand on the word and promises of God. Girl, you end up being unstoppable!

Prayer

Father, thank you for who You are and what You are doing in my life. I believe what You said about me. I make a conscious decision to stand on Your word. I believe you, God. Understanding that all things work together for my good. Nothing is impossible to me because I believe. So, as I think in my heart, so shall it be. The Lord is my light and my salvation. Whom shall I fear? Of whom shall I be afraid? On this will I set my hope. Praise shall continually be in my mouth, because you Prepare a table before me in the presence of my enemies. Always causing me to triumph. Blessing me with wisdom and knowledge. Leading me in the path of righteousness for your name sake. Everything I do shall prosper and I shall have success because with you I am UNSTOPPABLE! In Jesus name Amen.

About the Author

Erica D. Toussaint, the wife of one husband; mother of 3 amazing sons is a wonderfully charming, energetic dynamo. She is the catalyst that changes any environment she enters. Erica is an encourager, born with the gifts of edification, love and humility seasoned with an adamant belief that all things are possible to those who believe.

Being from the small town of Sunrise, Louisiana, the self-proclaimed *Country Girl* and *Meloh Chic* from around the way possesses a zeal for life that is hard for some from similar backgrounds to comprehend. Always one that can be found actively "putting in her work" the 27-year certified Human Resources strategist and CEO of ME Inc. Club is bent on making her own way while leveraging many of the learnings from her late mother. Her motto, mantra and favorite scripture and words she lives by come from the book of Mark 5:36 "Only believe!".

A Compilation by Donna Izzard

HARRIET ROGERS PRIDGEN

Unstoppable Story

I am unstoppable, intelligent, bold and a beautiful black woman inside and out. Intelligent, not solely based upon the degrees or certificates I hold, but possessing the intellect to know the obstacles of life are not deterrents to my goal.

Through my relentless pursuits, accompanied with my knowledge I have been shaped to step into my destiny unapologetically. It has given me the strength to take my power back from control, self-sabotage, abuse, rejection and insecurity.

I'm unstoppable because once I set upon a goal, an objective, a desire, I pursue until it's obtained. I may be faced with many obstacles as a woman but I show up each day in this world authentically thus amplifying my beauty. I am so proud to be a Black Woman.

Letter to My Younger Self

Dear Younger Me,

Can you believe the things that you allowed to hinder your destination? Days where you kept running through the maze of life and getting stuck at every corner. Do you remember when you were afraid to open your mouth and speak because of the laughs and giggles you received because you stuttered? I apologize for not fighting to give you a voice. I know it affected you and left you feeling alone, unable to fit in. Life has a funny way of making you feel isolated from the world as a young child. There were times you were angry because you could not go do the same things your friends were doing. You felt like you were in prison. I am sorry I allowed you to have those negative thoughts. Look at you now; you have a voice that speaks with volume and pride. Look at you now, you have grown past the obstacles that held you in bondage. I know life has been a struggle for you. You allowed fear to creep in and hold you hostage; too afraid to move through the maze of life. Congratulations! You faced your fears and kept moving, advancing to the end of the maze. You are now free to show the world your uniqueness. Your mind is at peace and you are the best you ever were. In the words of Bishop Jacqueline E McCollough: *"Your Feet are not called to be idle, but to fulfill the purpose and plan of the Father. But we must order our lives to ensure our feet are sturdy and ready for the work he has called us to fulfill for His Glory."*

Prayer

Thank you for traveling on this journey with me. My prayer for my unstoppable sister is that she continues to walk in courage. Father, remove any shame and guilt that is associated with her past. Help your daughter align properly with Your will in order to receive Your promises. Let her know she is no longer held by bondage; she is free to walk with confidence. Lord, break the chains of negative words that were once spoken over her. Remove the fear that keeps her from moving in her destiny. Don't allow her to be trapped by the excuses the enemy tries to plant in her mind; help her to only hear You. Father, open her eyes and allow her to see that you created her to be a woman of value and beauty. Let her rise up as the Black, Beautiful, Bold, Brilliant, and Business-minded women that you created her to be. In Jesus' name. Amen

About the Author

Harriet Rogers Pridgen was born and raised in the city of Philadelphia, Pennsylvania. She graduated from South Philadelphia High School. Harriet later moved to Burgaw, North Carolina, where she worked for the North Carolina Housing Authority for thirteen years. After leaving the housing authority, she became a North Carolina Correctional Officer, a position she held for eighteen years before retiring on January 1, 2021. She is currently employed as an Environmental Service Assistant at New Hanover Regional Medical Center. As of 2013 she serves as an advocate for abused and neglected children through the North Carolina Guardian Ad Litem Program. As a lifelong learner and woman of God, she earned a degree in Biblical Studies. She is also a licensed minister with multiple certificates in ministry, leadership training and substance abuse training. Harriet is an author, speaker, coach and Independent Travel Advisor. She has been featured on LifeHer Podcast show and featured in K.I.S.H. Magazine as one of the top 14 Extraordinary Women On the Rise. A devoted Christian, a wife, a mother, a grandmother a friend; confidant to many. It is her ultimate desire to open a transitional house for low risk offenders.

Contact:
Email: harrietprdgn1@gmail.com
Website: https://www.harrietpridgen.com
https://www.facebook.com/hrogerspridgen
https://www.Instagram.com/harrietrogerspridg

A Compilation by Donna Izzard

IFEYTAYA BULOW

Unstoppable Story

My name is Ifeytaya. I was born in Greenville, SC, but raised in Harlem, NY. As the oldest of eleven children, I consistently provided love and guidance to my younger siblings. I also have been blessed with two sons LeSean Bulow and Aaron Deck.

Because I love children so much, I also launched a successful day care center in 2002. As founder, I am still actively involved in the everyday administration and operations of the business so that it remains a viable part of my community. God has equipped me with strong leadership skills, and the compassion and sensitivity towards others to help me in the path He's given me to walk. Along the way, I get to encourage others and be His witness to those that cross my path.

I firmly believe this is the calling that God has given me to fulfill. I am grateful for His direction in my life.

Letter to My Younger Self

Dear Ifeytaya

There are so many things I want to tell you. It's difficult to know where to start. Life can be so amazing, and yet, at the same time difficult to handle. But you are so strong to get through the bumps in the road. I sometimes say you are growing much too soon. You have so much life to give. God has a plan for you. But right now, enjoy this time in your life. Enjoy having your health because you don't have things forever. Don't waste a second desiring to be older or somewhere else in life. Treasure this time because it goes by too quickly. You will see and experience things that will urge you to grow up too fast; don't let them. Cherish this time in your life and live every second as fully as you can.

Prayer

Dear Father God, I have been on my knees many times with my Bible in hand, tearfully reminding You of Your promises when my husband and I were in a dark place. Lord, the bible says: "They that wait on the LORD will gain new strength. They will mount up with wings like eagles. They will run and not get tired. They will walk and not become weary." Isaiah 40:31 Lord, many of my prayers have been centered on my own needs for a miracle. When I had enough of my marriage, and said I had enough, I felt in my heart that I should be gone and never return. However, the trauma in my life at that time hindered my prayer life. But after I humbled myself and cried out to you, Father, You delivered me from my distress. Amen. Thank you. I love you, Lord! Your daughter.

About the Author

Ifeytaya Bulow is a servant of God who has a love and compassion for God's people and the lost. She accepted Christ as her Lord and Savior at the age of 24. Her favorite scripture is Psalms 27 which states: "The Lord is my light and my salvation." Her desire to share God's love has had a life-changing impact on numerous people of all ages, gender, religion, cultural and social backgrounds. Ifeytaya is committed to her academic studies in human services and in the Word of God. In 2009, she received her Master's in Theological studies from Logos Christian University, and in 2016 was licensed as a Chaplain by Worldwide Association of Small Churches, and licensed as an Evangelist by Son of the Living God Ministries, Inc. In April 2021, Ifeytaya received her Doctor of Philosophy in Clinical Christian Counseling at Colorado Theological Seminary. Grateful for the direction of God in her life, she feels empowered and ready to follow God's guidance in expanding her role in the ministry.

A Compilation by Donna Izzard

JESSICA WILLIAMS

—✦✦✦✦✦—

Unstoppable Story

I'm an Unstoppable Black Woman because I didn't allow falling down to stop me from getting up! I'm created to keep going!

"Don't do it!" "Are you sure?" These were a few of the thoughts racing through my head. Faced with a decision, I answered with, "I do!" I often think back to the day I married my ex-husband. It's usually met with sadness. It reminds me of my disobedience to God. I chose to do a good thing, not a God thing. I had no idea who I was then, and didn't know who I would become. For years I had to live with the consequences of my disobedience to God. I cried and begged God to release me but it was to no avail. The day I said, "I do", I became a prisoner to my will, enslaved to my decision. But I didn't know this agony and mental abuse had a release date! I remember crying to God, as I often did, but this time was different. I told God if it was His will after 9 years I would stay but I was tired. I immediately felt a release and my chains fell to the ground. I now realize how important it is to wait on, and in God. I chose from my flesh but God appoints for your destiny. Now I wait on destiny. I know who I am and that makes me Unstoppable!

Letter to My Younger Self

Jessica, what you possess is valuable. Never allow anyone to diminish your value. You will never fit in because you were created to stand out. This will be a lonely journey and sometimes you will have to fix your own crown. Embrace your innocence. You don't have to be in a rush. Life is precious. Treat it as such. God is always with you!

Prayer

Unstoppable Black Woman, it's my prayer that you always incline your ears to God's voice. I pray you know that God is faithful and committed to His words concerning you. May you see God as Father and know that He extends to you another opportunity to do it His way. God, allow this beautiful, unstoppable woman to experience Your unfailing hand. Let her feel the rhythm of your heart in her life. While she waits to experience love again, be her greatest love story. Let there be an intimate exchange between You and her. Heal all of her wounds, Father, and bandage any open scars. Use her tears to water her secret prayers. Allow her prayers to manifest right before her eyes. Hide her as You heal her, Father, and shield her from embarrassment and ridicule. Be her protector and her peace. Forgive her iniquities and disobedience. Turn Your heart towards her. Restore, revive and rebuild anything about her that's been lost or torn down. And, Master, when You're ready present your masterpiece (her) for the world to see. In Jesus' name, Amen.

About the Author

Born on September 18, 1984 to Charles Williams and Deborah Lakin, Jessica was reared in the small city of Columbia SC, where she obtained her high school diploma from Columbia High School in May of 2002. Today, Jessica Latoya Williams is a business owner, licensed and ordained minister, motivational speaker, and spiritual Leader. Driven by her ambition and determination to meet the needs of others, Jessica takes pride in exemplifying servitude and humility in her devout role as Lead Pastor of New Nation Ministry Columbia. In addition to her role as an Administrative Consultant at The Department of Juvenile Justice, Jessica has also been recognized by the State of South Carolina for her degree in Biblical Studies from Destiny Bible College, as the CEO of Leading Lady Apparel LLC, as the founder of her nonprofit organization, The Journey, and for her sponsorship of " The Standard!! When boys become kings".

A Compilation by Donna Izzard

JOY HARRIS

Unstoppable Story

There is no condemnation for those in Christ. Yet, for sixteen years, I lived condemned. At the immature age of nineteen, I chose to abort a child. From then, I operated under a murderous spirit. I sabotaged and loathed everything that had the potential to live and flourish.

Guilt consumed me. Shhhhh, the church didn't make space for my confession. I suffered in silence; the enemy thrives and torments us in our secrecy.

I had a God call on my life at a young age but rejected the call because of my life choice(s). I labeled myself as unworthy and unloved. Shame stopped me from fulfilling my destiny.

Freedom came the moment I opened my mouth. I surrendered the negative labels and words. I embraced what God's Word said about me. I was not the choice(s) I made. Neither are you!

One in four have had an abortion. Are you one of the four? Are you entangled by guilt, shame, and condemnation suffering in silence?

Are you ready to move past the past, be free from bondage, and walk in overflowing joy? You can obtain healing and wholeness by accepting the redemptive power of Christ. Open your mouth and release your truth. Allow Holy Spirit to minister to your heart and heal the broken places.

That's what I did. I started sharing my testimony of how God restored my soul, [mind, will, and emotions]. Seven babies are alive because I came out of agreement with the enemy's lies.

Selah!

Letter to My Younger Self

Your unique outgoing personality is a gift to the world that will open unbelievable doors of favor. So never change who you are to appease others. Be authentically you! You are a world changer with destiny awaiting you. Do not allow choices to derail God's predestined path. Live without regrets. Choose wisely! Your voice is a powerful and effective weapon. Use it carefully to create life, expose evil, and speak truth to power. Speak boldly! Always remember that God loves you and created you to answer the world's question. Go be beautifully you! Give your whole heart to Christ and never give up!

Prayer

Yeshua, thank you that heaven recognizes me. Because of the blood of Jesus, I have abundant life, overflowing joy, unwavering strength, and God's peace. Every limitation in my life is gone, and I have the plan of hope Christ died for me to have. Seated in heavenly places, I see my life as God sees it. I am free from condemnation, guilt, shame, and live in His agape love that covers all things. I am fearless, making unstoppable impressions for the kingdom. Others' lives are better when they encounter me because I strive to serve and share as Holy Spirit instructs. I have a greater revelation because of the wisdom of God. My heart is pure because of the continued washing with the water of the Word. This is my year of exceedingly abundantly, and nothing can stop me...I am UNSTOPPABLE! I decree it is so in Jesus' Name.

About the Author

Joy Harris is a published author, International Speaker, and Award-Winning Coach at Authentic JOY, LLC. Over a decade, Joy's compassionate and interactive coaching style has made her much sought-after. An ordained servant, she empowers [Christian] women to achieve sustainable JOY, peace of mind, and productivity by creating a personal strategic JOY plan through her 90-Day Authentic JOY Coaching Program. She has brought hope and affirmative change to thousands. Her clients have overcome life challenges with confidence in Christ and feel internal peace and calmness. She encourages you to embrace the gift of greatness inside by challenging you to seek and live a joy-filled life; she empowers you to release the pain from past trauma and choices. Her passion is for you to live a thriving life overflowing with love. She moves you from being overwhelmed to overflowing with joy and peace. You "BEcome a JOY Carrier."

Connect with Coach JOY https://linktr.ee/authenticjoy

A Compilation by Donna Izzard

KARYN THOMPSON FARMER

———————❧❧❧❧❧❧———————

Unstoppable Story

"Congratulations, you are pregnant!" This news from my doctor was a tremendous surprise to me as a 42 year-old newlywed. Becoming a mother was a private desire of my heart, but I didn't think it was God's plan...but, He has perfect timing!

At seven weeks to my delivery date, my doctor said, "You have to give birth today!" Although traumatic, the birth was a success. I left the hospital two weeks before my child. I literally could not breathe on the ride home from the hospital. My experience with postpartum depression began. The mental anguish was often too much to bear. I was functioning daily but gripped with fear, anxiety, and weight gain. I withdrew from people and all hobbies that brought me fulfillment. I was trapped in my head.

Very few black women talk about postpartum depression. It's a silent mental illness, designed to cripple you and take the joy of motherhood away. I felt alone and ashamed that this was happening to me because I was perceived by all to be a strong and bold woman of faith. One day, I heard the Lord say, "Enough! Fight...I got you...this is NOT the end of your story!" That day I wrote down my strategy to overcome postpartum depression with God's help. I searched the bible for scriptures and became bolder day-by-day as I believed God for my restoration. Through much prayer, counseling and studying God's word, I am now living FREE – Faithful, Resilient, Extraordinary and Expecting.

Letter to My Younger Self

Dear Younger Karyn,

You are fearfully and wonderfully made in the image of our Lord and Savior Jesus Christ. Because of this, you have the power to overcome all things that come up against you. God gifted you with a Holy boldness, and that is okay. Please do not doubt yourself and do not reduce yourself to be accepted by others. Dream big and always be faithful; your faithfulness will produce greatness, if you are patient in the process. You will be devastated when your daddy suddenly passes away. Know that God will heal your broken heart. Give yourself ample time to grieve. Be intentional about balancing work and family. Use godly discernment in your relationships. The hand of God is upon you. You are uniquely gifted and prosperous. Remain humble and submissive as God elevates you. Sow into others and serve. Build it and trust God to enlarge it. Do not walk by sight! I love you, Older & Wiser Karyn

Prayer

Dear God, I ask that you comfort those of us who feel weary in well-doing. We try to juggle so many "hats", Lord, and often feel like we are not doing enough. Your word says that we are to trust in You and lean not on our own understanding but acknowledge You and You will direct our paths. We need You now to help guide us as we walk out our lives in accordance with Your will. Help us to embrace the unique characteristics and talents that you have given to us. We seek to please You with our lives. We desire to be women of noble character, and support each other to reach our full potential in you. Thank you, Lord, for entrusting us with your mighty work. May our kingdom assignments be fulfilled as You teach us how to walk boldly by Your Grace. In Jesus' name I pray, Amen.

About the Author

Karyn Thompson Farmer was born in New Jersey and now resides in Maryland with her family. She is a graduate of Hampton University (BS Math/Comp Sci), where she was initiated into the sisterhood of Delta Sigma Theta Sorority, Inc. Karyn is a cyber security professional, an entrepreneur and an active member of her church where she serves the Lord to empower women and children to live life FREE – Faithful, Resilient, Extraordinary and Expecting. She enjoys traveling, nature, exercising, teaching and financial stewardship.

A Compilation by Donna Izzard

KIMBERLY SHELTON

Unstoppable Story

"Keep It Moving" was a defense mechanism I used to suppress my pain. As a child, I suffered brutal molestations that were secret for many years at the hands of a family acquaintance, someone that people trusted. Who should I tell? Who would believe me? I was just a child...confused. This has happened to many of us, and most of us don't tell. I did feel in my heart that it was not right. It was also a way too common occurrence among us. This was a reality for many young girls in a place we called home. How sick is that?!

I felt hidden in plain sight. I believed the threats of my abuser when he said my parents would be killed if I told them what was going on. "Keep It Moving" became a way to cope. For many years, I navigated through life hurt, abused, violated, in fear, not trusting anyone fully, and yet living my life as if nothing happened. My smiles and laughs covered tears and pain for years.

I received Jesus Christ as my Lord and Savior when I was a teenager, and I found my voice. It was at this moment that I felt unstoppable. The promises that He made in His word, and the counsel I received gave me the confidence to speak into the lives of girls who had been through abuse. My faith in God's ability helped me to make "Keep It Moving" a mantra for never giving up no matter what life's circumstances may dictate.

Letter to My Younger Self

Dear Younger Self,

I hope that by the time this letter reaches you that my words will encourage your heart. I want to let you know how much you are loved and how thankful I am for you. You are beautiful, with beautiful deep brown skin, beautiful curly hair, beautiful almond shaped bright eyes, and a smile that lights up the room. You are powerful and can do anything that you set your mind to do. I encourage you to utilize every God-given gift you possess because it's going to touch and change the lives of others. You are necessary!

Prayer

Father God in the name of Jesus, I enter your presence on behalf of my dear sister. Father, I thank you for her life, and for the anointing that you have placed upon her to do exploits in Your name. I thank you that every life experience will cause her to hunger and thirst after You and Your word. I pray, Lord, that if she stands in need of a savior that she will have an encounter with You and receive You as her Lord. I decree and declare that her faith will move mountains and that she recognizes that all things are possible through You. I cancel the assignment of every word curse ever spoken over her and abort the enemy's assault. I declare that her purpose and destiny is being fulfilled and lives will be changed because dunamis power operates on the inside of her in Jesus' name.

A Compilation by Donna Izzard

About the Author

Finding the ability to endure this process called life, Kimberly Shelton has come to understand that adversity and trials are only opportunities for God to show Himself strong. Experiencing victory in these moments allowed Kimberly to testify of His greatness to many and propelled her into purpose. She is a servant leader who loves God, His word and people. She is a prophetic intercessor led by the Holy Spirit, and a teacher. Kimberly has a heart for under-served communities especially women who struggle from remnants of rejection, abuse, homelessness, and single parenthood. Kimberly has an unparalleled desire to help others change their generational trajectory, through God's word, encouragement, matriculation, and unshakeable faith. She has founded Operation S.O.W. outreach and the women's empowerment and prayer circle, The S.I.S.T.A.H.S. Movement. Her vocational background extends 37 years as an E.C.E and Elementary Educator/Director. Kimberly is a native of Brooklyn, NY, mother of two, and an entrepreneur.

Contact: iamKimberlyJ@gmail.com
www.thesistahsmovement.com
www.kidspiredacademy.com Coming Soon

A Compilation by Donna Izzard

KRYSTAL RYAN

Unstoppable Story

Both parents abandoned me. I was told that I would never be anything in life because my mother wasn't. I was molested from age eight to fourteen by my uncle. The only person that ever loved and nurtured me, my grandmother, died when I was just fourteen. I listened to my aunts, uncles, and my own father argue back and forth about not wanting to take me. So I wound up with my Aunt Geraldine, God rest her soul. That lady abused me every day that I lived with her because she blamed me for my grandmother's death. " If my mama did not have to take care of you, she would still be alive today," is what she told me. I was convinced that she was trying to beat me to death, but I survived that life thanks to my older sister Sharon. She called CPS in VA to rescue me in NC. Now grown, married, with two beautiful children, and yet again abused; I came out of darkness only to find myself in an even darker place.

I found myself in an abusive relationship for the second time. I had to run away again. I was homeless, jobless, with two children. I was alone in a new state where I knew no one. In spite of all this, and given the circumstances from which I had just escaped, I felt pretty amazing. This time I was determined to be led by God. I was a heroine. The strength I gained by walking out of my second domestic violence-filled relationship alive was only by God's grace. My children were worth living for. I found a church home before having a place to call our own. Both children finished high school and attended college. My son has never been in trouble; my daughter has a heart for God and is making significant moves in life. Me? Well, I finished school, got my degree as a Recreational Therapist, completed a business course, and became the CEO of Helping Hands Travel Companion in 2020. I am an Unstoppable Black Woman.

Letter to My Younger Self

Hey beautiful,

It is not your fault that you were abandoned. It is not your fault that your father was not there to protect you from the rape by your uncle. You still cry at times, and that's ok. God has a purpose for you Krystal. You were chosen to help change lives. Your pain is power. God chose you. You don't need anyone to say they are proud of you; be proud of yourself K. You suffered in silence. You sat in the closet for hours a day. It was meant to punish you, but it built you up. They thought you were talking to yourself, but you were talking to God. You will be happy, prosperous and make a difference in this world. You are undoubtedly one of God's masterpieces. Love, Yourself

Prayer

Father God, I come to you thanking you for my sister, God. My heart is filled with joy for the things that you have in store for her. Lord, her road may not have been easy. She may find herself in a place of giving up; maybe she can't see past the pain. I ask that You meet her where she is at this moment and wrap her in Your loving arms. God, when the path that she is taking seems unbalanced and scary, God let her remember in Jeremiah 29:13. "And ye shall seek me, and find me when ye shall search for me with all your heart." Remind her to put all her trust in you. God, I ask that You send the right people to be her support. Lord, remove those things and people that hinder her. I thank You for my sister's breakthrough. In Jesus' mighty name. Amen.

A Compilation by Donna Izzard

About the Author

Krystal Ryan believes that she was chosen for a purpose. Her passion lies in helping others to find common ground and the inner strength to escape from domestic violence and rebuild their lives not only for themselves – but also for those that depend on them. Krystal founded the Beyond Blessed Ministries outreach group in 2010 after escaping an abusive relationship and moving her two children from Texas to Denver. From there, the support group Through it all was born. Through a support group, web community, workshops, and community events, TIA helps domestic abuse victims and survivors connect, grow and learn from one another's experiences. Through Beyond Blessed, Krystal wants to be the outside person who helps others suffering from domestic abuse look within and gain strength and perspective. Krystal's mission is to create a safe haven where domestic violence victims and survivors can come together for support, resources, and more. A place to share their feelings and stories that they thought they never could.

A Compilation by Donna Izzard

LAKIA RUSH

Unstoppable Story

When I think of the phrase "Unstoppable Black Woman", I think of a girl who lived a life lost in the grips of depression, pain, shame, and hopelessness. A life filled with jail and prison cells, recreational drugs and alcoholism, violence and abuse, homicide attempts, suicide attempts, low self-esteem, low self-worth, promiscuity, and self degradation; a girl who chose to drop out of high school at the age of 16.

Then I think of how that same girl grew into a woman who slowly began to change her thinking. A woman who began to realize that she still had value and that she could do something different with her life. A woman who went back to school and got her G.E.D, a woman who graduated college with a Human Service Management degree. A woman who went to school and earned 5 life coaching certifications; a woman who started her own purse customization business. I think of a woman on a mission to unlearn every lie the enemy has ever fed her, and replace those lies with the promises of God. A woman who shares her story with anyone who'll listen, in hopes that it will encourage another woman to keep going despite the circumstances!

When I think of the phrase "Unstoppable Black Woman", I think of ME and how the challenges of my past were designed to kill not only me, but my purpose. Today, I'm humbled and grateful that God saw fit to grace me with chance after chance until I got it right! Now I'm ready to boldly move forward into what God has planned for me! I made the choice to become UNSTOPPABLE!

Letter to My Younger Self

Dear younger Kia,

I want you to know that you are beautiful, intelligent, and wise. I am sorry that your self-esteem and self-worth were sabotaged at such a young age which caused you to feel unworthy of succeeding in life. You no longer have to shrink who you are in order to fit in with your environment! You weren't created to fit in because God chose you to be different! I'm proud of you and I admire your resilience to push through the times that were designed to kill you! All of those dreams you chose to stifle because you felt you weren't good enough, I'm here to accomplish them for us with the help of God! P.S. I love you

Prayer

To every Unstoppable Black Woman that reads this book, I pray that God gives you the courage to pursue your dreams and goals. I pray that you see yourself through God's eyes and that you find the strength and courage to heal from the pains and setbacks of your past. I pray that you live a life full of peace that surpasses all understanding. I pray that God's grace, mercy, and favor will follow you all the days of your life! I pray that you stand on the promises of God and that you continue to strive to be all that you were created to be. You are an Unstoppable Black Woman! Embrace it, stand on it, and continue to walk in the greatness of who God called you to be! In Jesus' Mighty Name, Amen

About the Author

Lakia Rush is the CEO of The Plug's Daughter LLC., a Christian purse customizing company where she paints and embellishes purses with positive messages of faith, love, and hope. It is her belief that women have carried around negative baggage for such a long time (pain, hurt, shame) that she decided to create a different kind of baggage for them to carry with positive and uplifting messages. She is a college graduate with a degree in Human Service Management and a certified life coach with 5 coaching certifications in the areas of Happiness, Goal Success, Life Purpose, Professional, and Master Life Coaching. It is her goal to help women believe in themselves and understand that it doesn't matter how your story began, you have the power to change how it ends through belief in yourself and God's grace! Her motto is: "God is the plug, and I am the Plug's Daughter"!

Instagram: @theplugsdaughterllc_
Facebook: The Plug's Daughter LLC
Website: www.theplugsdaughterllc.net

A Compilation by Donna Izzard

MARCELLA D. MOORE

Unstoppable Story

Black, bold, beautiful, brilliant and business-minded. I remember every moment in my life that got me here. I open my eyes every day thanking God for life and embracing the gift I am, to the earth. The tears, disappointments, bruises and experiences all serve to empower me to empower others.

I show up in the world as a black single woman and mother who's been hit on every side. I realize that each hit is a lesson and each lesson births in me an incredible strength that at times amazes me.

To be honest, I've had many days when I wanted to tell God, "Never mind; You can find someone else to do my assignment." I actually tried it, but quickly learned that there is no escaping His purpose for my life.

Life is funny, often unpredictable and sometimes seems unfair, but we have been equipped to persevere and bounce back from all of the hits that come our way. You see, I discovered that just like the toy Weebles that were around many years ago, we as unstoppable black women, may wobble but we don't fall down.

I am unstoppable because although my wobble moments are many, I choose to live. I choose not to give up. I choose to embrace my own journey and I choose to honor the gift of me. I see every challenge and obstacle as an opportunity for God to show His amazing love, power and grace in my life. I am an unstoppable black woman. That's me!

Letter to My Younger Self

Hey Cella girl, I'm catching you at the beautiful age of 19 right before you got married and hopes and dreams were your driving force. I want to tell you that besides being confident, strong and a powerful leader, you are absolutely beautiful. The light that is on your life is powerful enough to cause transformation in the lives of many. Embrace your smile and voice because they will encourage broken hearts. Always honor the gift of you; follow your dreams, cultivate your gifts, never play small and don't get lost in relationships. Remember that you deserve God's best.

Prayer

Father, I thank you for your beautiful daughter who has grown into an unstoppable woman. I thank you for her trials and tribulations, her wins and lessons and for the destiny You have ordained for her life. I pray that You heal her broken heart and give her the wisdom to fulfill every assignment that has been assigned to her life. Help her to let go of what was, accept what is and bounce back to live a purpose-driven life. Help her to understand the power of forgiveness and the role it plays in her life. Holy Spirit, comfort her heart and remind her that she is loved. I bind every spirit in her life that doesn't represent You, and I lose good health, abundance, witty ideas, creative downloads, divine relationships, prosperity and long life. I pray Your good, acceptable and perfect will in every area of her life. Amen!

About the Author

Marcella D. Moore, affectionately known as "Cella D," is an Inspirational Speaker, Minister, Empowerment Coach, Mentor, Motivator and 5x Best Selling Co-Author. As the founder and Executive Director of Motivate and Pray, Inc. she serves and supports the community and other non-profits organizations while teaching about the benefits of using prayer as a strategy for spiritual development. As CEO of Marcella D. Moore, LLC she is dedicated to empowering women by helping them uncover purpose, identify and cultivate their gifts and talents and become change agents in their community. Marcella is motivated by her purpose-inspired message, "Be a part of your rescue, embrace your own journey, live on purpose, and love yourself to life." Her earnest prayers and desire are that the light of God on her life shines bright enough to make hearts open, babies leap and sleeping giants awake.

A Compilation by Donna Izzard

MARYANN JOHNSON

―――――ⓒⓖⓒⓖⓒⓖ――――

Unstoppable Story

My Unstoppable Black Woman Journey began in 1990. I got married early in life - 1981. My first child was born in 1982. My second child, a boy, was born in 1990.

The physical abuse did not start until after my daughter was born; then all hell broke out. I married my high school sweetheart. But he changed from the person I knew then into someone I did not know. He was physically, mentally , and emotionally abusive. It was not all the time but when it happened, I would have bruises from the fight.

I would always go back home to my parents with my daughter. And always, after a couple of days, he would come over begging us to come back home. He would always say there would be no more fighting, and that he loved his family.

That was the cycle of my life, which continued until September 1990. I'd had enough. I called my sister, Susie, crying on the phone and told her that there had been another fight the night before. I remember this fight like it was yesterday because I had picked up a knife and fought back. I wanted to cut his throat; there was fear in his eyes. The police arrived but I was not arrested.

My sister helped me and I left with the car, television, and clothes for myself and the children. She had a safe place for us to stay until I got my life in order. I left and never looked back. My ex-spouse died in 1992.

Letter to My Younger Self

Girl, you held on to your sexual abuse too long. Three men violated your body. But you kept silent out of fear. Yes, fear robbed you of your pre-teen and teenager years. You suppressed everything bad that happened to you. You needed help. Please, please forgive: live no more with fear. What happened to you is not your fault. You were not protected, and the devil thought to destroy you because of the physical and emotional violations you experienced. But God chose you. You are beautiful, bold, brilliant, business-minded and unstoppable.

Prayer

Father, thank you for your energy, might, power, and your straight strength. According to Ephesians 6:10, help me and every woman reading this, " be strong in the Lord and in His mighty power." As we trust in God's power rather than our own, You cause us to increase in new places. Almighty God you are my strength. You make my feet like the feet of a deer, and enable me to tread on the heights. (Habakkuk 3:19). As we pray and encourage others, Father God, strengthen the caregivers, family caregivers, who are caring for their elderly and chronically ill loved ones. They need Your help to prevent burnout and compassion fatigue. Thank you, Father God, for bringing me through to triumph. I can truly say, "Then I heard the voice of the Lord saying who shall send? And I said, "Here am I. Send me." (Isaiah 6:8)

About the Author

Maryann Johnson was born in Chicago, Illinois. She is a disciplined, hardworking professional who exhibits dedication to the nursing profession, and as a caregiver & life coach. Nursing is her passion. She often takes care of older family members providing exceptional care. After high school, she joined the Army in 1980. She completed her Associate Degree in Nursing at Triton College, ultimately receiving her Bachelor's of Science in Nursing from Lewis University, Romeoville, IL. She completed her Masters Degree in Nursing at North Park University, Chicago, Il. She is an Amazon #1 Best Selling Author of the book, The Ultimate Caregiver Guide - 20 Things You Must Know, which promotes health and safety in the home.

A Compilation by Donna Izzard

MEROLYN RODRIGUES

Unstoppable Story

Throughout life, you will be tested. If you believe in the healing power of prayer, you can successfully overcome any situation.

I am a bubble bath queen but, one dreadful night 23 years ago I decided to take a shower and had a horrible fall. I slipped backwards striking my head twice against the ceramic tiles. Unbelievably, I was conscious, sitting in the tub, the water raining down on my face. I remember touching my scalp to make sure it wasn't separated from my cranium. Suddenly I developed a severe headache. I knew that God was with me because I was able to get out of the tub and call a friend who took me to the hospital.

At the hospital they took x-rays and CAT scans. My brain was swollen from the concussion. I could not return to work and the following weeks I suffered from severe headaches and was prescribed additional bed rest. I always had a photographic memory and was already enrolled in Baruch College. On my return to school, I soon discovered that I could not memorize anything. I had to withdraw from classes.

My pastor, Creflo Dollar, encouraged me to stand on God's word for healing. Being a brilliant, bold, Black woman, I dared to believe and purchased his healing CD that covered every healing scripture from Genesis to Revelations. I listened and repeated the confessions daily for a two-year period interchangeable with Cindy Trimm's healing prayer. One day I realized I had received my healing. I could say every scripture without listening to the CDs. This was a big accomplishment.

Three years later I reentered college and completed my degree in Entrepreneur Management. I also earned a certificate in Project Management and several certifications in Floral Designing.

Letter to My Younger Self

Dear younger self,

You may not know this yet, but you are an unstoppable black woman who is destined for greatness. You will accomplish anything that you put your mind to and be successful in every area of your life. As you grow up, you may find it challenging to find friends that you can trust. Find that best friend in Jesus. When no one is around to listen or pray with, you can pray and talk to him. Never be afraid to let your voice be heard. You have a message to take to the nations. Love and believe in yourself, remember that you are beautiful. You are blessed with talents. Discover yours, and use them for the glory of God.

Prayer

Heavenly father I just want to thank you for today. Thank you for waking me up this morning with a conscious, right mind and for renewing my youth like the eagle's. Thank you for your grace, love and mercy. Before I was formed in my mother's womb You knew me. You knew the plans You had for me. You knew the times when I would be lonely, and needed a friend to confide in. You knew the times when I would need a friend to guide me so you gave me the Holy Spirit because you knew that He would be my closest friend. I stand on your word today and I plead the blood of Jesus over my body, over every situation, circumstance, and challenge that may come up today. I bind any satanic attacks and loose the angels to go forth and clear the path for me today.

About the Author

Merolyn Rodrigues is an accountant by day for one of the top financial institutions in the world. She is also the CEO of HTTS Floral and Event Designs located in New York. A certified luxury floral designer and event planner who provides services for all occasions. As a creative designer she curates memorable luxury experiences worldwide. "This Heir to God's seed", transforms space into magical, inspiring moments. Creating trendy, lush bridal bouquets, and large Extravagant designs of fresh and silk flowers are a promise. Continuously, investing in educating herself in floral and event design while building her skill sets for the floral industry.

Contact on Instagram and Facebook
@httsfloralandeventdesign
Phone: 917-533-4591
Email: heirtts@gmail.com

Website: https://www.httsfloralandeventdesign

A Compilation by Donna Izzard

MONIQUE ABUJANA

Unstoppable Story

My amazing story parallels the stages of a well known psychologist who developed a model to help teams of people progress through various stages to achieve their maximum level of performance. Similarly, as I have matriculated through life I have identified with the stages of forming, storming, norming and performing.

My 20s were a time of self-discovery as I sought my identity, and direction for my life. I had a near death experience and recovered not understanding the magnitude of God's purpose for my existence. I triumphed while forming because I stayed connected to God and continued to pursue my education and personal development.

In my 30s, after marriage, I desired to be a mother but was told that I would not be able to have children; however, God worked a miracle! I have been blessed with three beautiful daughters. I triumphed in storming while gaining clarity in my life for my purpose.

My 40s were full of highs and lows; transition was constant. I continued to be refined as I embraced opportunities for growth and leaned into God for wisdom, guidance and strength. I triumphed in norming as my daughters were my priority and my parental philosophy is, "I only have one time to raise my children and I'm going to do my very best with God's help."

The fabulous 50s? Well, this is my time and my place to perform, produce and prosper! I have been prepared to share my "Bs" with the world!

Letter to My Younger Self

Dear Monique,

You have consistently been a kind, considerate person! You have always presented your genuine self and assumed others did the same. You learned to discern the authenticity of others while determining their place in your life. You will grow up and impact the lives of many young people, especially your three daughters. I will suggest that you continue to put God first in every area of your life. Take advantage of opportunities presented to you to grow personally, spiritually and academically it will result in you prospering financially. Never give in, never give up! Sincerely, Your Younger Self

Prayer

Heavenly Father, I come humbly to thank You for the opportunity to share this prayer with my sisters. Father, you are an unstoppable God! Your Word declares that You made us in Your image, after Your likeness; so therefore we are unstoppable! We thank You for every promise given in Your Word that we boldly declare and decree that we walk in...... Joy, Help, Hope, Love, Power, Peace, Grace, Mercy, Plans, Favor, Wealth, Refuge, Wisdom, Safety, Courage, Comfort, Healing, Dominion, Strength, Kindness, Presence, Guidance, Patience, Blessing, Goodness, Salvation, Provision, Direction, Atonement, Gentleness, Protection, Redemption, Long life, Revelation, Prosperity, Good things, Restoration, Deliverance, Graciousness, Faithfulness, Eternal life, Self-control, Satisfaction, Relationship, Transformation! Father, I seek the kingdom of God first, and Your righteousness and all these things will be added to my life. In Jesus' Name I pray! Amen.

About the Author

Monique Abujana is an educator, financial professional, speaker and coach. She has served as a principal, assistant principal, curriculum generalist, teacher and coach over twenty-five years committed to helping students in her area acquire high quality education while being instrumental in the growth and development of other educators. She has received her formal education in Finance and has paired her extensive experience in academia and financial knowledge with passion to help educate families on how to secure a solid financial future. She speaks on culturally responsive practices in schools, school reform in a pandemic and beyond, teacher and administrator development, and effective parenting strategies while navigating the K-12 experience. She also speaks and conducts seminars and webinars to educate others on building a financial legacy. Monique Abujana is the CEO of Dominion Financial Services and offers an array of financial services to individuals and businesses and is completing her doctorate in Educational Leadership. She is a fifteen year veteran of the United States Army Reserve where she served as a trainer. She is married to Joseph Abujana and together they have five children.

A Compilation by Donna Izzard

MONIQUE WHITE

———⚬⚬⚬⚬⚬⚬———

Unstoppable Story

It was 2002. I finished law school and accepted a clerkship. However, the 2002-2003 judicial clerk salary was pitifully low. I had a mortgage and a child to support. But... I had a plan. I would continue nursing. I realized the problem weeks after I started.

> *"A law clerk shall not hold outside employment aside from teaching, lecturing, or writing."*
> **— Code of Conduct For Judicial Employees, Canon 5B(3)**

My heart sank. Anxiety built. If I couldn't work as an RN, I had to resign. I needed to speak to the judge ASAP. Thereafter, I petitioned the division. I appealed to the vicinage. I escalated it to the Director of the Administrative Office of the Courts. Such an arbitrary rule without considering individual facts and circumstances placed an undue financial burden on law clerks with a chilling effect on recruitment.

I won that fight but didn't realize it's impact. While visiting the judge years later, his secretary introduced new staff. She sought out the law clerks. I was perplexed until she told them, "She's the reason you are allowed outside jobs now." I was shocked. She turned, "You didn't know that, did you? They changed the rule because of you." My personal fight had statewide ramifications. The revised rule reads,

> *"Superior Court or Tax Court law clerks shall obtain written permission of (a) their judge, and (b) the Assignment Judge, ... prior to taking outside employment; ...."*
> **— Code of Conduct For Judicial Employees, Canon 5B(3)**

My persistence and determination impacted thousands.

Letter to My Younger Self

Dear Monique, God has chosen, blessed, and set you apart. You are in this world but not of it. Trust your intuition. You are stronger than you think. When you feel like giving up, press. Those times will be your defining moments. Resist the urge to play small. Boldly take your place. Never chase after friendships or relationships. You are not meant for everyone. Everyone is not meant for you. Ignore the distractors. When you're told that you are not enough, agree. You are more. When they say you can't, show them how. Unapologetically. Black. Beautiful. Brilliant. Bold. Business-minded.

Prayer

Gracious Father, Thank you for my unstoppable sister. Thank you for granting her divine health. Thank you for empowering her to step on serpents and scorpions and over all the power of the enemy. Thank you for sending out your armies before her. I pray that you strengthen her to stand steadfast, immovable as she walks her path in power, love, and with sound mind. Shield her from every fiery dart of the enemy. I come against all forms of negativity, discord, strife, and distraction. Quiet every tongue that rises up against her. Show every lie spoken to be false. Grant her peace in the midst of every storm. May the works of her hands be blessed. May the fruit of her womb be blessed. May her borders be enlarged, and her storehouse overflowing. Be it unto her, Father, according to your word. In Jesus' name. Amen.

About the Author

Monique White is an attorney, registered nurse, certified professional coach, international speaker, Amazon bestselling author, and founder of Triumph Services LLC, a consulting and coaching firm. As a transformation strategist, Monique helps professionals monetize their expertise to transform their circumstances to live as God has promised-with love, joy, hope and power. It is her mission to break chains and transform lives.

A sought-after speaker, frequent podcast guest, and host of the shows Real Talk and Chrysalis Effect™, Monique has been described as visionary, anointed, driven, encouraging, and persistent. Whether she is speaking at a conference or workshop, being a panelist, consulting on business or legal matters, or just holding a patient's hand; Monique's passion for propelling and empowering others shines through. She is truly a leader who serves.

Connect with her:
Website: www.triumphsvcs.com
Facebook: www.facebook.com/triumphsvcs
Instagram: www.instagram.com/triumphscoach
Join the Group: www.facebook.com/groups/womentranformed
www.facebook.com/groups/transformedentrepreneur

A Compilation by Donna Izzard

NENA B. ABDUL-WAKEEL

Unstoppable Story

Every morning, on my way to work, I stopped at 7-Eleven to get coffee. A medium coffee with amaretto creamer. Ty was always behind the counter. A young black man with a ready smile and charming personality. Like normal he had a new question for me about computers and networking. But on this particular day I had a load of books for him. I told him, "the best way to learn is by doing. These should get you started." 2 years later he started his own business. He reminds me every time I see him that I was the one who believed in him and helped him get started.

When I was younger, I was shy and felt overlooked and discounted, because I was dark skinned, short and plump. People didn't seem to expect much from me. It was very discouraging. As I got older, I realized I never wanted anyone to feel what I felt. Everyone has value, purpose and promise. So I always tried to speak positively to people. I soon realized they weren't just nice words, but words "given" to me to speak. I was being used by God to encourage people. Imagine being chosen to say something that can change the trajectory of someone's life.

Ty is just one example of the many people I have encouraged to pursue their dreams beyond their current circumstances. And each one of those people are able to help someone else. That's unstoppable. I'm proud to be an UNSTOPPABLE ENCOURAGER.

Letter to My Younger Self

You are a rare gem. I wish I could tell you that you won't have hard times. But that wouldn't be true. But you do have something inside you that is beautiful, brilliant, bold and unstoppable. Like a diamond, some of your best qualities will come from the pressing and even pain. Keep going. DON'T STOP. When others seem to be ending, you will just be beginning. You won't be late; you will be right on time. In God's time. Don't be afraid to shine. That's what diamonds were meant to do. When you feel dimmed, take a moment to rest. Know that you will shine again. Shine on.

Prayer

Lord, thank you for your purpose and promise. Thank you for putting your Spirit on the inside of me. Thank you for the Spirit that won't let me quit even when my mind and body wants to. Thank you for the Spirit that reminds me that I have an assignment on my life. Strengthen me when I am weary. Calm me when I am frustrated. Inspire me when I am discouraged. Remind me that You love me. Remind me that You are always there. Remind me that You will supply all I need. Send me Lord. Send me Lord to inspire. Send me Lord to reassure. Send me Lord to encourage. Send me Lord, in Your Name. Amen.

A Compilation by Donna Izzard

About the Author

Ms. Nena B. Abdul-Wakeel is the Founder of Social Media Success Network, and a national speaker on simplifying social media for entrepreneurs and career professionals. Her specialty is LinkedIn. A pivot point for her was the 2016 release of the movie "Hidden Figures". She realized that she was a hidden figure and decided to stop being invisible and bring her own spotlight. Today she's focused on helping others do the same. She specializes in helping leaders leverage LinkedIn for visibility, credibility, and influence. Nena's core passion is supporting and inspiring others to experience success in their lives. As she aspires to create success in her own life, Nena is always mindful of the advice she gives to others; "*Be Encouraged. Be Empowered. Walk Boldly into Your Dreams. Because you are Great!*" Nena is an Amazon Best-Selling author, award-winning actress and mother of two very talented boys and resides in Silver Spring, Maryland. Connect with her on LinkedIn or learn more at www.msnenab. com.

A Compilation by Donna Izzard

OBIOMA MARTIN

Unstoppable Story

I believe what the bible says I am. I believe what the bible says I can do. My faith in God makes me unstoppable. My faith in myself makes me unstoppable. I believe in myself and I believe in God who created me. He is the author and finisher of my faith. I can do all things, and all things are possible with God. God has equipped me with everything I need to accomplish everything He has given me a vision to do. Greater works is what I am called to do, and greater works is what I set my intentions to accomplish. I move, live, and excel because I am made in the image and likeness of my Maker. I cannot fail, cannot stop, will not stop. It is my desire to represent my heavenly father. Failure is not a part of my DNA and that is what makes me unstoppable.

Letter to My Younger Self

You are unstoppable because you are made in the image of your Maker, the almighty God, the Author and Finisher of your faith. Anchor yourself in the Word of God. Do not take things or what others say or do, personal. Do not wear your feelings on your sleeve. Put all confidence in God. Put no confidence in man. Trust God for He is all you will ever need, and He will supply every need. God is, and will always be your source. Focus on all things and people that are life giving and purpose driven.

People are not going to understand you, get you, like you, support you or acknowledge you. Allow their ignorance to continue to fuel you. Never give up on your dreams and goals. Never settle for anything less than God's best. Let go of your agenda; focus on God's agenda. Be still; become prayerful. Pause before you move; pause before you respond. Pause so you can breathe. Pause so you can think and allow oxygen to go to your brain so you can make intentional decisions and not decisions rooted in emotions. Your emotions are your gauge, not your guide. Allow the Holy Spirit to lead and guide you in everything. Focus on God's unconditional love, grace, mercy and forgiveness. Become quick to listen and slow to speak. Invest in You. You are amazing.

Prayer

I decree and declare that you continue to draw your strength from the ultimate power source. May your cup never become empty. I pray that you will continue to soar and sow from your overflow. I decree that whatever you decide to do, it shall be done according to your faith. I decree that God increases you in supernatural favor, wisdom, knowledge, and understanding. I pray that nothing and no one shall come in between you and your divine appointments and relationships. I pray that you remain steadfast and ready in season and out of season. I ask for all these things and better for you in Jesus' name.

About the Author

Obioma Martin is an international transformational speaker, trainer, conscious cash flow activist, accountability-coach, author, and esteemed advocate for women's empowerment. Martin's passion for equipping women with the tools they need to, not only survive but prosper and live audaciously, has launched her into a life of unparalleled servitude, wherein she continues to thrive by helping others. She is the founder of several organizations that serve the under-served in the community: OmazingYou is the publishing company and produces all informational products, events and apparel. OMART -Women Supporting Women is the Not for profit arm that focuses on providing battered women with children and teen parents with safe housing, workforce development, life after trauma and other supportive services and programming. We support survivors of domestic abuse and provide opportunities for them to start businesses and return to school.

Martin has developed over 5000 women and transitioned them from welfare to earning credentials required to complete and further their education. A life-long learner herself, Martin holds multiple degrees; associates in Early Childhood Education, Bachelor's in Childcare Management, a master's degree in Early Childhood Education and Leadership, Goldman Sachs 10,000 Small Business Program alumni, certified biblical counselor, and ordained evangelist.

Contact Martin at info@omazingyou.com
Follow her on FB@omazingyou
IG @omazingyou
Twitter @iamobiomamartin
Podcast @anchor.fm/obioma-martin
Website www.omazingyou.com

A Compilation by Donna Izzard

REBECCA D. HUGGINS

Unstoppable Story

For with God nothing shall be Impossible, Luke 1:37.

From a child, I knew that I was different. I had an innate desire to be successful and have a higher quality of life. For me, quitting was never an option; therefore, I relentlessly pursued success. However, to have a good life, I accepted Christ into my life, and learned and applied the Word. God's word and my determination helped me become the Unstoppable Black Woman I am today.

I was driven to matriculate through the educational system by graduating high school and then obtaining my Bachelor's, 2 Master's and completing several doctoral courses which have been crucial to me receiving promotions in my career. I have been able to positively impact the Secondary Educational Arena as well as start a thriving and profitable business and ministry.

Secondly, my faithfulness to God has helped me to become the Unstoppable Black Woman that I am today. Specifically, throughout the years, I have devoted time to learning and applying the Word of God to every aspect of my life. Additionally, I have consistently tithed and sown offerings into the Kingdom of God since I was 19 years old and I am reaping the benefits of being a tither.

In closing, I was determined to be successful and God has helped me to become an Unstoppable Black Woman who is faithful and driven to be all that He created me to be.

Letter to My Younger Self

Dear Rebecca, I want you to know that with God you are destined for greatness. Don't be concerned about trying to fit in because you are a precious valuable commodity who was marked for greatness while you were in your mother's wombs. You may lose some people along the way; be okay with it. Hold your head up and don't succumb to the pressures of the world. Instead keep your sight on the Kingdom of God and His way of doing things. He will supply everything that you need to succeed in life. You are a generational curse breaker and you are birthing nations in your bloodline. You will leave a mark on this earth which will never be erased. Keep serving, keep loving, keep pushing because you have an anointing and the power to change the world.

Prayer

Dear Father, I come boldly to the throne of grace. I thank you for my sister's life. Your word says that my sister is fearfully and wonderfully made in your image, and everything you created is good. Abba Father, when my sister was in her mother's womb, you crafted a plan and purpose for her life. I decree and declare that abundance is my sister's birthright. No lack shall ever come nigh her dwelling place or family. Everything she touches shall prosper and every place the soles of her feet tread belongs to her. Wealth and riches are in my sister's house. Her husband, children and grandchildren call her blessed. She is an innovative 21st century leader who is making investments, acquiring property, and has sound wisdom fully operating in her life.

About the Author

Rebecca D. Huggins is a 21st Century Leader, bestselling author, 26-year veteran middle level educator, speaker, Leadership Strategist, The Content Innovator, Host of the Authentic Conversations Podcast, and the CEO of Leader's Circle University, LLC. Rebecca assists her partners in creating their social media content, serves visionary authors, writes their books and creates their online courses. As a result of partnering with Rebecca, her clients experience an 85% profit in their business. Additionally, Rebecca is the host of "The Serve Experience" a conference for servant leaders which assists authors, coaches, consultants and organizational and ministry leaders in monetizing their gifts in the marketplace. She is the founder of the Content for Profits: Servant Leaders Arsenal. Rebecca is the mother of one daughter, Andre'cia Simone and "glamma" to one grandson, T'zion Karter. They reside in Columbia SC.

A Compilation by Donna Izzard

DR. RENE MINTER

Unstoppable Story

It was the first day of classes at my new school. As I drove onto the university campus I noted riding stables and students with their riding attire mounted proudly like this was an everyday activity. I parked my Nissan amongst a sea of Mercedes and BMW's. The grounds, immaculately manicured, were beautiful with tulips in various colors cascading the landscape like something I had only seen on a postcard.

Hurrying about the campus, I stood out; there were no other black faces to provide kinship. I arrived at the class early after checking the roster on the door to ensure my name was there. I took a seat in the back of the empty classroom and waited. I thought I would be judged solely based on the melanin in my skin.

Students started entering and taking their seats. There was a buzz of excitement as students asked if anyone knew the professor. I could feel my heart racing as class was about to start. Everything was predicated on this moment, but I had earned the right to be there even as the only black face in the room. I shook the fear fueled by systemic racism as I stood up and walked to the front of the classroom. With the weight of my ancestors from slavery to present I took a breath and said, " Good afternoon, I am Professor Minter". Mouths agape in shock meant nothing to this unstoppable black woman for she had arrived!

Letter to My Younger Self

Dear Younger Self,

If you only knew of the incredible life you will have you would count it all joy, understanding that your struggles are not closed and locked doors. They are merely opportunities for God to show Himself mighty on your behalf. Keep dreaming as there are expiration dates on your dreams. You will find education to be your great equalizer even as black child in a white school. Keep studying and believing. Treat all with respect regardless of how you are treated. Do not be afraid to entertain angels. Always walk in faith showing God's love to all. Remain humble and kind, always letting God's light shine through you. With the utmost admiration and gratitude, Me

Prayer

To my beautiful black, bold and brilliant sister, I come before the Father thanking Him for the creation in you. I thank Him for placing greatness in you. It is my prayer that you will come to embrace the magnitude of all you are and all you can be. It is my prayer that you will hear the voice of God and allow Him to shine through you. It is my prayer that you be comforted by the Savior as well as being a comfort to those who follow in your footsteps. Know that you carry the dreams and passions of others who came before you. Never doubt your greatness as you were wonderfully and uniquely made by God.

About the Author

Rev. Dr. Rene Minter is a Christian Based Psychotherapist in private practice in New York and Director of non-for-profit management. She is an advocate for mental services where she treats patients in need without regard to income. She believes " All Minds Matter. " She is a social worker by profession with a master's degree in Clinical Social Work and also possesses a Doctorate in Ministry. She is devoted to the ministry of missions globally with projects in West Africa where she offers charitable support to women and children. She is the television host of 'The Miracle in You with Dr. Rene' on the Believe in Your Dreams Network. She is the author of 6 anthologies; Women Inspiring Nations, Your Voice Matters, Women who Pray and Amazon #3 time international best seller; Finally Free, Drop the Mask, Share the Crown and Thankful and Blessed 365. She is an Author, Blogger, Motivational Speaker, Humanitarian.

A Compilation by Donna Izzard

ROSIE THAMES

Unstoppable Story

Many of the experiences you have in life as a woman will leave you doubting yourself and have you feeling defeated. Am I doing the right thing? Am I making the right choices? What are people saying about me? These are questions that plagued me in the past. I felt like I was just "winging" this life, wandering aimlessly with no purpose. I was serving my country in the United States Air Force; I was a wife, a mother, and a successful entrepreneur, and yet I still felt like there was a HUGE void within me. Something was missing; I felt absolutely miserable!

My breakthrough came in a way I would never have imagined. Frankly, if I had a choice I would have opted for a different method. God took me through the valley and a series of back-to-back storms for seven years straight. There was a crisis in my marriage that left me broken; my husband was diagnosed with renal failure at age 34, losing his military career as a result of his illness; I lost my mom when she was only 56 years old; my son was in the ICU for two weeks from pneumonia and a collapsed lung, and I was seven months pregnant, dealing with the demands at work while being a caretaker at home, and then some. It was a lot to endure but it was in those moments I learnt something significant about myself...I AM UNSTOPPABLE!

These things that the enemy sent to destroy me only made me stronger and more resilient. Why? Because I trusted God throughout the process. I realized that God was using these storms to develop something in me that couldn't have happened otherwise. Now I have a story to tell. I use my story to encourage other women to embrace and endure the storms and challenges that life brings and empower them to tell their UNSTOPPABLE story!

Letter to My Younger Self

Dear Rosie,

I want to write this letter to you because I know exactly what you are going through this very season in your life. I know things seem difficult, you may feel misunderstood, unloved, abused, misused. The hurt and the pain is tearing you apart. You wonder if you will ever escape the chaos and if a brighter day will ever come. Well, believe me, that day will come and in ways unimaginable! Don't lose hope, keep pushing, and hold on to the promises of Isaiah 41:10, "Fear not, for I am with you; be not dismayed, for I am your God; I will strengthen you, I will help you, I will uphold you with my righteous right hand."

Prayer

Loving Father, thank you for the phenomenal, beautiful, unstoppable black woman reading this prayer. Let her see herself as you see her - as fearfully and wonderfully made. She is your gift to this world. Thank you for creating her for such a time as this to be a vessel and to be used by you to impact the world. I ask that you equip her for the mission she was assigned to accomplish. Grant her favor and give her success for the journey ahead. May she prosper and never lack anything good, may her storehouse be filled to the brim and overflow. I declare Ephesians 3:20 over her life "exceeding abundantly above all that she can ask or think." May she overcome EVERY obstacles, outlast EVERY challenge, and come through EVERY difficulty better off than she was before. Use what the enemy meant for evil and turn it around for her good. Amen

About the Author

Rosie Thames is a devoted wife and mother of three phenomenal children. She is a 20 year combat veteran in the United States Air Force, a servant-leader, mentor, best selling author, publisher, coach, speaker, successful entrepreneur and an overcomer. Hailing from Kingston, Jamaica, Rosie's passion is to impact lives, bring hope, healing and transformation by empowering, inspiring and motivating others to live their best life and dream big. Rosie and her husband Rich are the 2020 Eagle award winners in their business, a prestigious award and the highest award given to the top producing leader within a given year. They launched Growing 2 Greatness LLC and Team No Limit, teaching people how to leverage the direct sales industry and earn a significant income from home, become debt free, and live life on their own terms. Her vision is to empower others to succeed despite adversity and inspire people to leave a legacy for generations to come. She coaches entrepreneurs by using the strategies and methods she used to grow her own business and develop herself as a leader.

Connect on Instagram and Facebook @RosieThames

A Compilation by Donna Izzard

SCELETIA EVANS

――――――∽⌒∽⌒∽⌒――――――

Unstoppable Story

Though my life has been filled with many blessings, I am most thankful for my son, Ashton. Before I successfully had a son, I had multiple losses. How many losses you ask? Sadly, five. After loss number two, I became angry and bitter. Mostly with God. After all, wasn't I taught that God hears our cries and gives us the desires of our hearts? Why not me? Am I not good enough? Am I unfit to be a mother?

Typically, after a loss, a professional will come into your room. In my case, it was an angel. "Why do you weep?" she asked. I gave her a look that was filled with unpleasant thoughts. She came closer to my bed and said, "This is God's way of protecting you. He's still sitting high, and all power is in His hand. Dry your tears my sister and know that you are walking in His purpose. Be anxious about nothing. It's just not the right time for you. My heart was too raw to comprehend her message at the time. I left the hospital still in despair. I wanted to hope but I doubted that I'd ever obtain success.

During multiple stays in the hospital, I befriended a nurse named Georgette. She checked on me daily. Two weeks passed. Georgette called and shared a need for her ministry. Her organization provided grief counseling to people who have experienced loss. I was baffled when I received the request to share my stories. Honestly, I felt I needed help. My character will often say "yes" even though my heart says "no."

The invitation was accepted. After the completion of my formal training, I became a grief counselor. I had never given thought to the strength found in grief. We've all experienced loss in some way. We each deal with loss in different ways. I was obedient and have gained reward far beyond anything imaginable. This includes the successful birth of my now, fourteen year old son, Ashton. Never give up, never give in, stick with God's purpose and you will always win.

Letter to My Younger Self

You won't know the path of your life. There will be days filled with beauty and others filled with strife. At birth, your grandmother prayed and covered you with His blood. Always, remember how much you are loved. Your star will shine bright, so much so, some might not appreciate the brilliance of your light. Don't be discouraged by their hurtful words. Stay vigilant knowing there is a God above. Take time for fun and be willing to share; as your life is filled with riches, you'll have plenty to spare. Keep God first in everything you do. Trust me, younger self; the Master will see you through. Life will be filled with moments you might not understand. Walk in faith knowing God has a master plan.

Prayer

Dear Heavenly Father, I humbly come before You today with thanksgiving in my heart. I am grateful for Your touch that gently woke me this morning. Father, thank You for allowing me to serve in Your word another day. I thank You, Lord, for giving me abundant peace for You know the things that trouble me deep within my heart. Thank You for being a magnificent counselor and an omnipotent God. Lord, I ask for Your forgiveness of the wrongs that I may do and of which I am not aware. Teach me, Lord, how to forgive others as You have forgiven me. I ask that You pour into my mind the light of Thy Truth. Help me Lord to spread your word and be a vessel to those in need. Lord, I find peace in knowing You are ever so present in my life. If I knock, You'll answer; If I seek, I shall find. I am asking that You always help me to make wise decisions and stay on the path of my ordered steps. These things I pray in Your name. Amen

A Compilation by Donna Izzard

About the Author

Christian | Mother | Business Owner | Friend

The above words are a brief description as to who I am. As a Christian, I remain on ready, set, go! I take pride in being a soldier for Christ knowing that people are my passion. I was born in a small Mississippi town on September 10, 1970, to Ethel & Willie Smith. Throughout my childhood I was shown the true meaning of unselfishness from both my parents. Their countless measures of love, patience, and guidance were an amazing example. Therefore, I've carried this example into my journey of motherhood. I hope to remain a source of inspiration to my son. I embrace all of the B's, Unapologetically! However, I identify the most with being Business Minded. I am the proud owner of two small businesses and I manage several Logistic Operations companies. In addition, I continue my second love: I strive to empower ladies with the importance of health education that is crucial to overall happiness. As a friend I maintain compassion with an open heart. Always willing to celebrate the good times and providing an ear, shoulder, or tissue during the struggles. I'll sum up my Biography by stating, "This is me, Unapologetically, Sceletia."

A Compilation by Donna Izzard

SHIRLEY TOLIVER

~~~~~~~~~~~~~~~~

Unstoppable Story

I am not sure when it started. It may have been when I was eight years old and busted my lip resulting in a knot on my lip forever. It may have been when I realized I was of darker hue. It may have been when I noticed that I had rounder hips. Maybe it was because I experienced being touched in places where little girls should not be touched. It may have been the series of dysfunctional relationships. Or it may have been the abortion that's still hard to share.

At some point perfection became my portion; it was natural to excel within the corporate landscape because perfect people do not often have to share the REAL.

One must be perfect through micro and macro aggression experiences. Perfect through the denial of advancement, and in August 2020 perfect through the impact of, "Your role is being eliminated effective January 31, 2021". The next morning, instead of my usual alignment with GOD I opened my eyes remembering that exact phrase from the day prior.

GOD asked me a question: "Daughter, remember how you have always referenced your impending exit like this?" "If GOD's willing, I will retire in 2023". Daughter, did you really mean that all those times or was it something you said habitually?"

As I write this, just two days prior I responded "no" to a habit. My contribution to this work is the first of many future experiences and decisions that line up with Jeremiah 29:11. Prosperity is not habitual; it's my future by faith with courageous and bold actions meant to dominate within my sphere in the marketplace, my relationships and my business.

Letter to My Younger Self

Young Shirley you were always enough; able to take risks, be bold and carry it differently. Perfect people are ordinary. Prosperous and hopeful people are different in most ways. GOD has always had his hand upon you. Jesus loves you so much that He whispered your name when he said, "It is finished for Shirley". The Holy Spirit literally grieves when you are hurting and longs to comfort you. Your gift is heavy but you are anointed to carry it. You have been anointed for a Purpose since the day you arrived on earth. Take what belongs to you and refuse to carry that which does not perfectly align because it constricts you.

Prayer

Unstoppable Black Woman I pray that you walk in the promise of a future full of the hope, prosperity and experiences that are your portion from God. I pray that your gifts continue to be released. I pray that you dominate in the space that God has created for you and that you are the catalyst that helps other women and men dominate within their appointed spaces. I pray that your faith in God removes the anxiety of going bigger and bolder. I pray that the Holy Spirit never leaves you as you courageously become more resilient with the plan that God has set for you. I pray that you remain strong spiritually, emotionally, and mentally. Unstoppable Black Woman, I pray that your past does not continue to negatively impact your present and that your future is more than you could dream or think.

A Compilation by Donna Izzard

About the Author

Shirley Toliver is a People Builder heavy in the DE&I space with HR tendencies. She is a Senior Human Resources Practitioner and has spearheaded award winning Human Resource teams throughout the US. She is frequently recruited to facilitate Women Employee Resources, Business Resource and Affinity Group programs providing leadership and relationship building strategies often combined with customized training programs. Shirley is the founder and Chief Power Officer of Life On Power, a global women empowerment project that encompasses the brand "What if She knew She was Powerful". Through Life On Power, Shirley provides programs, resources and coaching to individuals and groups. As a personal development and executive leadership coach, Shirley is an inner power and purpose strategist. Shirley's message always encompasses fulfillment in lieu of happiness. Happiness is an emotion and fulfillment is soulful leading to healthy self-awareness.

Connect on Instagram @shirleyltoliver and @ lifeonpower on Facebook @shirleytoliver

On the web www.lifeonpower.com

A Compilation by Donna Izzard

STAR M. HOLMES-WORD

Unstoppable Story

My Great-Great-Grandmother Georgia Jones, affectionately known as Nana, was an Evangelist and Psalmist. She recorded a gospel album and my family always said that she wrote the song Precious Memories, but never received credit for it. From the stories I've heard, she was a remarkable woman who helped those in her community struggling to feed their families and passed the baton of love, faith, and entrepreneurship to her two children: my Great-Grandmother Vera and my Great Aunt Marge.

My Great-Grandmother Vera, known as Mama, was a leader in her church and her community and I recall seeing many clippings about her in the newspaper about the acts of kindness she had done in her community. She too passed the family baton of faith and love.

My grandmother Yolanda was a hustler! She owned several businesses which were my up close and personal introduction into the world of entrepreneurship and provided me a great deal of insight into black women in business and building relationships with vendors.

My mother has been a social worker, a cosmetologist, a beauty salon owner, and she co-owned a boutique with my grandmother. Over the years I learned that she and my grandmother endured much trauma in life but thankfully, did not allow the pain from those experiences to interrupt the baton pass.

Mom passed the baton to me. I too endured trauma but decided to heal from the pain and make sure our family baton pass remains unstoppable. As a mother of two boys and one girl, this unstoppable black woman knows that family is important and is on a mission to pass the baton of faith, entrepreneurship, and healing to the next unstoppable black woman in our family.

Letter to My Younger Self

You weren't wrong. Every fearful time that man came into your room, it wasn't your fault the adults didn't protect you. You smelled his unforgettable scent which will trigger you for years to come but it's ok now because God made something good from the bad. You will help hundreds of women cope with similar triggers, nightmares, self-blame, and feelings of powerlessness. You will take back your power. Hard as it will be, you will forgive your grandmother. How? By accepting Christ as your Lord and Savior and understanding that Christ paid the price for your sins. You being forgiven made it easier to forgive others. You are unstoppable.

Prayer

Thank You, God, for healing our hearts and making us unstoppable black women who know the importance of pausing to deal with the generational and personal trauma in our lives. We know it is You who places us in spaces that provide the tools and resources to heal from the pain. No matter how many times we have fallen we will continue to get up and lead our children and community. We will choose ethical behavior and let Christ's light shine through us. We know that on our own, we are not perfect but we continue to strive to be the best that we can be. Because we are unstoppable black women, favored by God, we will speak up when we see others doing wrong and we are confident that our voices will make a difference. We are daughters of the King and we are unstoppable.

A Compilation by Donna Izzard

About the Author

Star M. Holmes-Word is an Author, Jewelry Designer, Speaker, Advocate and Life Coach. Star coaches other women coaches who have also experienced trauma in their own lives on how to effectively stay connected to their clients when they themselves experience triggers. As A Domestic Violence/Sexual Assault Advocate, Star received level three training through the Coalition for Domestic Violence and sexual Assault Advocacy in Des Moines, Iowa. She has helped over 150 DV/SA Survivors, as an Advocate (during divorce proceedings) assisting survivors with safety planning, securing Orders of Protection, helping women understand the dynamics of power and control, the effects of trauma, and healthy relationships. Star looks forward to continuing to share her voice all over the world and helping women move from the back to the front of the line!

You're A Star Too Enterprises
615-586-7873

A Compilation by Donna Izzard

STEPHNIE A. EDWARDS

Unstoppable Story

I've spent a lot of my adult life surviving; meaning, most of my adult years were met with what seemed like continuous stumbling blocks, and many storms. There were many moments when the days ahead seemed grim but somehow there was a light inside of me that kept pushing me to be optimistic. As a woman of faith, I have learned that God allows us to go through situations to grow ourselves even when it does not feel like growth is happening. Despite my circumstances and feelings of brokenness, I did not break.

I continue to experience challenges that require me to not only break old habits but to view them as opportunities for self-development. I now wake up every day with a renewed spirit, determined to live each day one day at a time. These changes helped to transform my inner self and have resulted in a positive and humble mindset. I count it as a blessing that through prayer, I can listen to my inner voice to guide me to make the right decisions. I remain self-motivated and find ways to let go of anything that creates a toxic environment. I have learned the importance of connecting with like-minded people who can help mold and shape me into an unstoppable woman, and help me see new possibilities and opportunities. Life is filled with obstacles and it is important that we position ourselves to work on creating an atmosphere that will allow us to overcome and build confidence.

Letter to my Younger Self

Dear younger self,

There is more to life than simply surviving. During my early years, I was unsure about myself and ignored many of my passions. I received a government job after completing high school because it was secure. I want you to know that the feeling in your stomach is a sign to take action. You can figure out the things that bring you joy and make an income from them. Your purpose will find you when you make the decision to take a step outside of your comfort zone. Until then, I am proud of you and you are unstoppable, even if you do not feel unstoppable just yet. With love and support, Stephnie

Prayer

Heavenly Father, I thank you for a new day, for the opportunity to wake up with a renewed spirit. Lord, I ask that You remove the enemies of progress from these women of God. Give them strength when they are weak and the spirit of courage when they are in doubt, so that they can see the vision that You have ordained for them. Lord, I ask that You bless them with the spirit of wisdom and pour into them testimonies that they can share with others. Lord, comfort them as they meditate daily on Your word so that their spirit may be filled with passion and creativity to execute the gifts that you have given them. Lord, let them continue to seek Your guidance as they stand in the gap for their families. I pray for their continued protection, in the name of Jesus Christ our Lord and God. Amen

About the Author

Stephnie A. Edwards is an administrator, entrepreneur, designer, author and mentor. She aspires to inspire others and does so by leading by example, demonstrating possibility in the face of obstacles, positivity in the face of criticism and enthusiasm in the face of despondency. Stephnie actively engages in self-development and improvement. She is a Certified John Maxwell Team Member, a member of Toastmasters International and holds a degree in Organizational Management, from Ashford University. Stephnie is also the CEO of Stephnie Edwards, a jewelry boutique, created with the vision to help women feel beautiful and confident about themselves. Stephnie's contributing chapter to the Unstoppable Black Woman Project, "Broken But I Did Not Break", shares her experiences on overcoming challenges, breaking old habits and reaching for her dreams. With her motto of "stay focused", she believes that nothing is impossible. The sky's the limit once you reposition yourself to soar.

Learn more about Stephnie Edwards, visit www.stephnieedwards.com.
Instagram: @stephnieedwards.ceo

A Compilation by Donna Izzard

TENNILLE THOMAS

Unstoppable Story

Born to a hardworking, single, black unstoppable young woman, dedication and strength was my birthright. I was always considered bossy because of how I dealt with my peers. I am extremely direct and I know what I want. But I wouldn't say I was bossy; rather, BOLD. In high school, I planned to graduate early so I could start college early. I remember having many meetings with my guidance counselor regarding my schedule. She constantly advised against schedule changes, but I had to be my BOLD self and let her know *I got this!* I sacrificed, graduated from high school early, and began the journey to find my career. I felt proud; unstoppable. Nothing broke me.

I enrolled in a private college to study media communications, which I loved, but hit a roadblock. The out-of-pocket expenses and student loans were more than I could handle, so I had to withdraw. I felt like a failure. But I had to remind myself that I was an unstoppable black woman full of promise and purpose.

Becoming a single mother and raising a young queen, I decided to go where my brain and skills would take me -- nursing. I also worked full time and became very knowledgeable as a healthcare professional. I was blessed to become a wife and now a mother of three. But I never forgot my first love -- creativity. I now have my own podcast, I am a published author, and I'm back to writing daily.

Being an unstoppable woman means that although I may have chosen a different route to get to my destination, there is no shame in that. It's a unique route I created and now I'm back to doing what I set out to do so many years ago. For all of you unstoppable black women reading this, please stay on your journey. Don't let fear or procrastination take what's for you. I promise the reward is sweet.

Letter to My Younger Self

You are a force. Never doubt your vision or dreams. Stay with God; He loves and knows you best. I am so proud that you did not let people steal your joy and courage. You stayed secure even when faced with molestation, abuse, and unkindness. None of that made you see yourself as broken or unloved. Tennille, some adults would have folded under what you went through, but you didn't. I know these things happened to you because early on you knew God for yourself and believed He was your salvation. The devil often seeks out young believers like yourself to break you and destroy your faith in the Lord. However, whenever you had doubt, you received words from His angels that would help you fight back defeat, grief, and struggles. Do you know how blessed you are Tennille? The goals and dreams you had for yourself, your Father continues to see them through. For He knows that little girl will grow to move mountains, teach her family about Him, and mature in His word so that his light can shine through.

Prayer

Heavenly Father God, please bless all my unstoppable sisters. Cover them with your blood, Lord Jesus, and reveal their true purpose here on earth. I pray that they grow in faith and trust God to lead them in times of uncertainty. Let them know they are an unstoppable force with so much to offer. Create a circle of unstoppable women around them who can be strong for them in times of weakness. Help them love their children and loved ones so hard that the evils of this world can't break past their love and prayers for them. Oh, Lord, I pray this unstoppable woman knows she has the strength to build a relationship with You as priceless as life itself. When you say YES, Heavenly Father, who can tell her no? Cover her, dear Lord from the crown of her head to the soles of her feet. Amen.

About the Author

Tennille Thomas is an RN, Podcaster, Writer, dedicated Mother, and Business owner. She is the CEO of FlourishingT LLC, which is a brand just as much as it is a business. She has been a healthcare professional for over 16 years, and is in demand, providing expertise and advice on various health issues. As a Christian woman with a strong faith, Tennille, is just the influencer needed for women today.

Podcast: "Get the Tea on Life with T"
Connect on Instagram and Facebook: FlourishingT
Website: flourishingt.godaddysites.com

A Compilation by Donna Izzard

TIFFANY NANCE

—————⌒⌒⌒⌒⌒—————

Unstoppable Story

Life can catch us by surprise when we least expect it. That is exactly what happened to me when I heard that "C" word that nobody wants to hear. Cancer, this horrible disease that is supposed to happen to anybody but me. We pray for others to be strong, courageous and healed in the mighty name of Jesus when they are diagnosed but can we execute that same belief system and energy for ourselves? Instead of asking God "why me?" I channeled those emotions into becoming the unstoppable woman that would interrupt cancer's life instead of allowing it to interrupt mine. Doctors told me that the cancer would not respond to chemotherapy. I knew in the inner depths of my soul that it would. I could see a glimpse of my future and that was enough for me to know that my story would not end this way. Yes, I prayed for healing and strength, but I also told God that my life had purpose and there was so much more of it left to live. Of course, God already knew this, but he needed me to say it to show I believed it. As months of chemotherapy, surgery and daily radiation treatments robbed me of my hair, appetite and energy, I embraced baldness, gained weight instead of losing it, and worked every day. I was determined to not look like what I was going through. Cancer was served a death sentence. Not me; I am unstoppable.

Letter to My Younger Self

Dear Tiffany,

You are ready to make your mark in this world. You have it all planned out; college, graduate school, a great job and a family. Know that it's okay if things do not go as planned. Sometimes what you plan, may not be what God has planned for you. Challenges will come; some of them will change your life forever, but always have faith and trust that the Lord will see you through. Know that you are put on this earth for a purpose and your purpose will be fulfilled.

Prayer

Most gracious and heavenly Father. Lord, I honor and thank You for who You are in my life. It is through You, God, that all things are possible. I give all praises and glory to your holy name daily. Thank you for being that still voice that tells me You have a path for my life. Thank you for being my strength and courage when I was weak or afraid. I see Your unconditional love for me in every aspect of my life and I just want to say thank you, Lord, for loving me and showing me how to love. As I look back, Lord, I thank You for sparing me and allowing me to have another chance at life. As I look forward, Lord, I know that You are right here with me.

A Compilation by Donna Izzard

About the Author

Managerial consultant and visionary behind Nance Tax Service and TDN Training and Consulting, Inc. With over 20 years of experience, she brings a wealth of knowledge in management, coaching, banking and delivering financial education to individuals and businesses. Tiffany has a heart for empowering women to reach their fullest potential. She is a breast cancer survivor and mother of two wonderful sons; Jeremiah and Myzale.

Tiffany holds a Master of Business Administration and a Bachelor of Science in Management and Organizational Development from Bethel University.

A Compilation by Donna Izzard

TINA M. WESS

————— ⚬⚬⚬⚬⚬ —————

Unstoppable Story

The Unstoppable Black Woman? That's me! The rising of the real B, Black, Beautiful, Brilliant, Bold and Business-minded to become the Unstoppable Me!

All of my life I have been unstoppable. I knew when I was a little girl that I was special in a good way. One of my grandmother's friends told me at the age of 5 that God had a special calling on my life and I would do great things for His name's sake. That statement has been with me all of my life. I knew I was different from the other kids because I didn't do the things that they did. Fast forward to college, and then adulthood. I have always been brilliant, bold and business-minded, not to mention beautiful. I am not conceited, just convinced. I had my daughter in 1992, and then twins 1 ½ years later. Then I became a single mother and raised them alone. I knew I had to be unstoppable and show them how bold I was. My daughter tells me all the time she wants to be half the woman I am, and I tell her, "No, you want to be better than me." She said, "I am not sure if that is possible." In 2017, I had a stroke with hemorrhaging at a church healing service. God said, "You will go through some things but you will be fine." To God Be The Glory. I went through the fire but was not consumed. I am UNSTOPPABLE.

Letter to My Younger Self

Dear Younger Me,

You are worth so much more than you think. This is something you will struggle with. You will think you're not good enough but I promise you are. You are so much more than enough. Stop looking to others to find your worth. Learn to love who you are and let that be enough. Know that you are God's beautiful creation and nothing you achieve in life or fail to achieve will ever change His love for you. You do not have to be perfect. It is an illusion.

Prayer

Dear Lord, I come before your throne of grace to say thank you for uniting us as unstoppable black women so that we can serve you and accomplish your plans in this world. It is not easy for women to come up together for a common purpose without there being any trace of strife or contention. Lord, give us strength to be able to stand firm as one, and fulfill the plans you have set before us. Strengthen us in our inner being that we may be able to overcome all the attacks. Amen.

A Compilation by Donna Izzard

About the Author

Tina M. Wess is a motivational speaker and entrepreneur. She is a single mother of three young adults and newly promoted to GiGi in March 2021 of her first grandchild. I have a daughter and twin boys. Her life as a single mother is her fuel to speak to women who feel their lives cannot be lived as planned because now they are alone and have dual roles in their households.

Her motto is "She was born with everything needed to live out her God given purpose. But what she has been given is not just for her so she has to share and touch lives of others with her God-given skills through sharing her experience. Email: wessconsulting17@gmail.com

A Compilation by Donna Izzard

TRACY MITCHELL-TURNER

Unstoppable Story

To all of my melanated queens, repeat after me:

"I am an unstoppable black woman! I am bold, brave, and built for greatness! I possess the creativity and productivity to manifest my destiny and live life to the fullest! "

The unstoppable black woman has mastered the art of advancement while facing adversity. From Madam C.J. Walker to Madam Vice President Kamala Harris, being unstoppable has been intricately woven into our DNA. We carry the resilience and tenacity of our ancestors who refused to allow slavery, gender inequality, illness, and poverty to stop them in their plight for dignity and respect. My mother taught me that an unstoppable black woman owns the beauty, value, and genius she possesses. She speaks with authority, walks with confidence, works with integrity, and lives life on her terms.

Unstoppable black women are unapologetic and uncompromising in maintaining their core values. We choose us FIRST by prioritizing our worth, wealth, and wellbeing. We cultivate, collaborate with, and celebrate each other 365 days a year. We schedule time to relax, recharge, and renew so that we can show up fully. We are changing the narrative on how others see us and how we see ourselves by writing and directing our own stories reflecting more positive images on the screen. We remain committed to uplifting our unstoppable black men and giving back to others.

Unstoppable black women harness courage and discipline and recognize the meaning and significance in their existence. Being unstoppable is not about perfection but rather ongoing course correction when we fall short and mess up. We refuse to allow past failures, pain, and rejection to define us or discourage us. We promise to support unstoppable black women with the tools necessary to maintain momentum, when needed. We will hold each

---

other accountable. No matter what, we will not stop!

Letter to My Younger Self

Dear Tracy,

God has equipped you with a voice to empower women. Do not be intimidated by your small stature. Your confidence will cause your presence to stand out. You will fail but it's not final. Keep going and you will succeed. People will hurt you. Forgive them and release the pain. Making straight A's, overcoming peer pressure, writing stories when you are bored, and having tough talks with your mother seems irrelevant now, however, these experiences are shaping you into the woman that you are destined to become. Cherish these special moments as the best is yet to come!

Prayer

Heavenly Father, I lift up my unstoppable black sister. I pray that she will obey the voice of God. I pray for her to repent of her sins and renew her mind daily. I pray for her to consistently speak words of life and encourage herself in the Lord. I pray for her to be healthy and whole in her physical body. I pray for her spiritual, mental, and financial growth and development. I pray for her to be fruitful and multiply in every area of her life. I pray that she will choose faith in God over fear of man. I pray that she will seek purpose over power and fulfillment over fame. I pray for her strength that she will not grow weary in well-doing. I pray that she will use wisdom and discernment in decision making. Help her to remember that, "No matter what, I will not stop."

A Compilation by Donna Izzard

About the Author

Tracy Mitchell-Turner is the founder & CEO of Tee Mitchell, LLC. She is a Registered Nurse, Bestselling Author, Certified Life Coach, Speaker, Wife, and Woman of Faith who resides in Atlanta, Georgia. Tracy empowers leaders, coaches, speakers, and entrepreneurs in personal development, business acumen, and public speaking. Tracy is the author of "SONKISSED: The ABC's for Blessed Success" and co-author of "You Need It, I Got It." Tracy has been featured in The Huffington Post, The Real Georgia Peaches Documentary, and Good Deeds & Spotlight Sister Magazines. Tracy helps women discover the hidden value and limitless potential in everything they possess (skills, talents, abilities, and experiences) and create the life and business they desire. Tracy is equipped with the skill sets that enrich women physically, mentally, spiritually, and emotionally resulting in healing and wholeness. Tracy enjoys speaking about life, biblical wisdom, business, fashion, and wellness. Tracy can be reached at the following: www.teemitchellspeaks.com, Tracy@teemitchellspeaks.com, on Facebook at Tracy Tee Mitchell-Turner, and on Instagram at @teemitchellspeaks.

A Compilation by Donna Izzard

VIOLET STEVENS

Unstoppable Story

I was the woman with the alabaster box in Luke 7:37. I had become the sinner, the harlot. The one who was gossiped about and belittled growing up. Demeaned, judged and ostracized. Written off and tossed aside. She was exactly who I identified with. This nameless woman in the Bible who is known by two things: her implied sin and her act of attrition. Here she was, unworthy of mercy; consumed by judgment, and lost.

I had succumbed to the weight of these labels throughout my life. They became my identity and in spite of my accomplishments I was undeserving of love and unwilling to be loved. This was who I had become. Desperate for salvation and love. I saw myself in her. Dr. Sean McMillan said, "People will judge you on speculation, but God will love you with concrete evidence." Jesus looked at that broken and ostracized woman and shut out the noise. He saw what she truly needed.

And He then said to the woman "THY FAITH HAS SAVED THEE, GO IN PEACE." The final words of that passage resonated within me. I think that the most important thing for a broken, hurt and lost person to be granted is peace. I was always led to believe that peace is the absence of strife and turmoil. Peace, true peace, is actually defined by the tranquility provided WITHIN the strife and turmoil. Seeing myself through His eyes restored my vision and made me Unstoppable.

Letter to My Younger Self

Hello Beautiful,

You are bigger and brighter than the world you see around you. Never shrink or dim your light to make others comfortable around you. There will be times when people will tell you that they love you, but love is an action word. They will not only speak love. They will breathe love. No one will ever love you more than you love yourself. You must love yourself so well that it encourages people to rise up and match it. You are not and will never be less than. You are capable of doing the extraordinary. Shine Baby.

Prayer

Romans 12:2 says, "And be not conformed of the world, but be ye transformed by the renewing of your mind, that ye may prove what is that good and acceptable and perfect will of God". Father God, I thank You for loving me in spite of the enemy telling me otherwise. You have called me and named me as Your own and I am the apple of Your eye. There is no force on earth that can keep me from becoming what You have created me to be. I declare and decree that no weapon formed against me shall prosper for it is by Your will alone that I move, speak and grow. I place all that I am at your feet and speak life over all that I touch. Success and abundance is my portion. It is so In Jesus' Name. Amen.

About the Author

Violet Stevens is an avid advocate for self care and serial entrepreneur located in NYC. She is also a wife and mother who believes that the recipe for Black Girl Magic is resilience, love, pride and faith. It is through this belief that she feels others can be encouraged to not only persevere through the tribulations of life, but expertly navigate the halls of colleges and boardrooms as well as the world. Her belief is that her words will inspire others to release themselves from the shackles of shame and labels to walk in their true God-given authority.

.

Made in the USA
Middletown, DE
16 July 2021